MW01247839

1,000 Creative Writing Prompts for Holidays: Festive Ideas for Blogs, Scripts, Stories and More

Bryan Cohen

DEDICATION

I dedicate this book to the many days of school I was not able to take off for holidays and the teachers who kept me focused on the learning at hand.

CONTENTS

FOREWORD

In August 2010, I compiled two years worth of material into a book called *1,000 Creative Writing Prompts: Ideas for Blogs, Scripts, Stories and More.* The material took the form of writing prompts, story starters that can help writers of all ages to turn an idea into a story. I'd written those prompts every now and then while I was working various jobs at offices, coffee shops and eventually, my freelance writing career. Surprisingly, the book of prompts, which was more of a last ditch effort to get me out of debt than an attempt anything substantial, began to take off.

Two years later, I've decided to start writing prompts more often on a variety of subjects. I have the opinion that every aspect of our lives can be mined for creativity. This book and the other ones that I plan to follow it with will help you to start digging.

Personally, I think that's all you need from me to get started, but I love my original introduction from *1,000 Creative Writing Prompts* so much, I've decided to include it here. Take a look for some tips on how to use the book, an idea for a 30 day writing plan and some other tidbits of wisdom.

No matter where you are in the "trying to be a writer" process, I hope that this book helps you to take the next step. Happy writing.

Sincerely,
Bryan Cohen
Author of *1,000 Creative Writing Prompts*
August 2012
http://www.buildcreativewritingideas.com

INTRODUCTION

My name is Bryan Cohen and I want to help you write. I'm the author of a website called Build Creative Writing Ideas and I'm also the author of this book.

I've found that one of the toughest things for a writer to do is to come up with ideas and so I've created *1,000 Creative Writing Prompts: Ideas for Blogs, Scripts, Stories and More* to help writers avoid this dreaded writer's block that I keep hearing about.

A prompt is a jumping off point that helps you to get your brain and pen moving. Some of these prompts are questions, some are scenarios and many of them deal with your own life and memories. When you use a memory or an emotion to write from, it helps you to feel like you aren't starting from scratch. There are thousands of stories already in your brain and many of these prompts are attempts to jog your memory and to use your brain for all it's worth.

I also feel that when you use your memories and your heart for these prompts, the writing ends up coming from a place of great truth. Even if you are writing a fantastical story about a boy and his dog, if it comes from a foundation of honesty, the story will strike a chord with your readers. Successful franchises like *Harry Potter* work for a number of reasons, but I believe the main reason is that we relate to those characters. Creating from truth is the first step to successful writing.

I'm proud to say that these prompts are original and that I've put many, many hours into coming up with them. I've gotten some extremely positive feedback from users of my website and so the creation of this book was the next logical step. I've written a few short essays to help get you started, but you can start writing from the prompts right away if you wish. So…hop to it!

How to Be a Writer

A lot of people feel like they need some kind of permission to be called a writer. Like once they've taken enough classes or once they've published something there is some tribunal that will decree that they are now in fact writers. Others feel as though they're writers even though they've never even made an effort to write more than a short story here and a poem there.

We live in a tough world full of put-downs and negative talk. If someone does not have the will or the ability to achieve his dreams he may feel the desire to kick around the aspirations of other people. We may hear this kind of unproductive negativity from our parents, friends, loved ones and those we mistakenly see as our enemies.

A writer is a person who can see through all this negativity and still feel passionate about writing. A writer wants to write and wants to figure out ways to make writing more a part of his life. There are some writers that are financially successful and others who haven't made a dime, but they are all still writers.

If you say over and over again that you aren't qualified enough to be a writer…you will fulfill your own (kind of boring) prophecy. If you tell yourself that you are a writer and you tell other people this over and over again, the opposite will be true. But how do you know if you're a writer?

If you aren't sure if you qualify as a writer, there is only one thing you need to do.

Write. Just write. Write as much as you can as often as you can. It doesn't matter if you've written anything lately, just start now. If you have an off week, month or year, it doesn't matter because you can start writing again at any time. If you have the desire to write and you can give yourself the permission to have this passion in your life then you are a writer.

This is about the time that the excuses come rolling in:
"I don't have enough time."
"Writing doesn't pay and I'm broke."
"I don't have any motivation."

Solving these problems is as easy as visiting your local library. Hundreds of books have been written about time management, financial management and creating motivation in your life. Continuing to make these excuses and ones like them, with solutions available at any time (for free, no less) is essentially laziness.
Laziness is boring. A life of spending your free time watching television and learning everything you can learn online about celebrities (or the like) is boring. If you even have an inkling of wanting to be a writer, pick up a few books that will leave your excuses in the dust and try working hard to make something of yourself.

My website, Build Creative Writing Ideas has many tips and tricks to improve your motivation and time management, so if you can't get off your butt to visit the library check it out. For those of you who are ready to write, strap yourself in and try a few of these prompts on for size. Happy writing!

How to Write from Prompts

These 1,000 creative writing prompts have been compiled from various ideas that have floated in and out of my head over the last two years. I have made as many as I can very open ended so that the same prompt could be used multiple times over.

The prompts often take the form of a scenario with a question:
"259. You see a little boy wander into the middle of a busy intersection. What do you do?"

There are multiple ways that you could choose to write from this prompt. You could launch into a first person story or explanation:
"I would immediately drop all of my belongings and run to his safety. As I run into traffic, my life would flash before my eyes and I would hope desperately that I could make it to the boy in time to save us both..."

You could make it into a third-person fiction story:
"Derrick and Joey laughed and sipped their drinks. All of a sudden, Joey noticed something out of the corner of his eye.
"What the..."
Joey trailed off as he noticed a young boy trip and fall in the middle of the road. He was all alone. Joey was the only person with enough time to act..."

Or you could transport it into another genre:
"The boy tripped and fell in the middle of the road. The truck struck him with all its force and it quickly shattered into a million pieces. The nearby cars screeched to a halt and stared with their mouths agape at the uninjured boy."

What you write from these prompts could be the start of an entire story or it could just allow you to get a few paragraphs in for the day. You could write a blog post based on what you write, a short story, a poem, a teleplay, a screenplay, a stage play, a novel or anything else that requires putting pen to paper.

These are not assignments by any means. You can write as much or as little as you wish. Run with an idea until you can't think of anything else and then try another one. Write one story from a prompt and then write a completely different story from the same prompt. What you use these prompts for is up to you. If you turn one of these prompts into a million-dollar screenplay (and I hope you do) go off and enjoy yourself, because I will not expect anything from you in the slightest. I created these ideas so that writers could simply write from the heart without having to think too much so go off and make me proud.

If you don't like a prompt, you don't have to write from it. You can also come up with a new prompt based on the prompt you don't like. Seriously, whatever you want to do with this book and these prompts, please feel free to do it. I just want you to write! If you ever have a question about where a prompt came from or what I meant by a particular prompt, feel free to contact me on my site, Build Creative Writing Ideas.

Writing Every Day

One fantastic way to use this book is to write from one prompts every day to keep yourself trained and fresh. Writing every day can be difficult to get started but once you make it a habit it'll be just like flossing (except much less gross).

The method that I like to use to integrate new habits into my life is a method developed by blogger Steve Pavlina called "The 30 Day Plan." One of the mistakes people make when trying to add a habit to their lives is that they think too far down the line wondering, "How could I possibly make this a habit for the rest of my life?"

Steve Pavlina recommends that you look a lot more short term. He likens adding a new habit to installing some software with a free 30 day trial. Try adding a new habit (like writing the prompts) to your routine for just 30 days. Choosing this time constraint allows you to easily block the month off in your calendar and it doesn't feel too overwhelming to just think about four tiny little weeks.

The best thing about "The 30 Day Plan" however is that 30 days is as long as your brain needs to make a task into a habit. You have slowly but surely trained your brain into writing a prompt every single day and now it's already a part of your life. This makes it a much simpler task to keep writing a part of your day.

Find a time of day that you almost always have free. This time should also be a part of the day that you are energized and awake. If you always get home from work tired, you may not want to choose the ten or fifteen minutes right when you return. The time should be specific and consistent. I enjoy writing in the morning after I've gone on a jog and I've had a light breakfast. Another reason I choose the morning is because if something comes up, I have the rest of the day to find time for it.

Set a clear goal for yourself. Some people set a word count per day or set it at one page per day. To start out, you may just want to require only a few sentences per day to get in the swing of things. An example of a clear writing goal is:
"I will write 200 words from a different writing prompt each day at 8 a.m. for 30 days starting August 1st."

Once your goal is set, all you have to do is start. So hop to it and let me know how it goes. Thanks so much for trying out *1,000 Creative Writing Prompts*. I wish you all the writing success in the world.

Sincerely,
Bryan Cohen
Author of *1,000 Creative Writing Prompts*
http://www.BuildCreativeWritingIdeas.com
August 2010

LABOR DAY, ROSH HASHANAH AND COLUMBUS DAY

LABOR DAY

1. Labor Day is a holiday meant to celebrate the hard work that people do all year long to help keep the country moving forward. Who are some people you know who work hard every day at their jobs? Why do you think the work they do is important?

2. For many students, Labor Day is the last holiday before school begins. During Labor Day, are you excited for school to begin or do you wish the holiday lasted for the entire year? Why?

3. Over a hundred years ago, people who worked in jobs had to work much longer days with fewer benefits for their families. Why do you think it was so hard for workers to get rights for themselves and their loved ones?

4. If you could have any job in the world, what would it be and why? What are some of the things you'd have to do to get such a job?

5. Of all your relatives and family friends, who do you think has the most interesting job? Do you think he or she enjoys the job or that it's just a way to pay the bills? Why?

6. Which do you think is harder, work or school? What are some of the things that make work more difficult and what are some things that make school tougher to deal with?

7. Imagine that you and your friends have been sucked forward through time 20 years into the future. In this future, all of you work at a office job for a big corporation. What is the office like and how do the other people there seem to enjoy it?

8. Describe the most difficult job you can think of. What are some of the tasks people who work there have to do? Do you think that the job is important or not important and why?

9. Create a made-up story using the following words: paycheck, job, alarm clock, and suit.

10. One of the best parts of Labor Day is that it's your family's last chance to go on vacation before school. What is your ideal family vacation? Why would that be perfect fun for the whole family?

11. What do you want to do for a living when you grow up? Why would you enjoy that as a job? What would your back-up plan be if the first one didn't work out?

12. How do you think you could best honor the hard-working people of the world? Would these working folks appreciate your kind gesture? Why or why not?

13. Imagine that your parents gave you chores to do as part of an allowance. What are some of the chores you might have to do? How much would this hard labor be worth and why?

14. Some of the toughest workers in the world are the ones who save lives, like doctors, firefighters, and police officers. What do you think it would be like to save people as part of a job? Why might the job be especially difficult?

15. Labor Day is all about relaxing after engaging in a lot of hard work. What are some of the things you do to relax? Why are these things so relaxing?

16. Create a dialogue between two factory workers an hour before the end of their shift on the day prior to Labor Day. What would the two of them talk about and why?

17. When workers feel like they aren't being treated right, they can form a group and go on strike. What would it mean for the business if the workers were to go on strike? Do you think a strike is a good idea? Why or why not?

18. Picture your favorite toy or game. Imagine all of the steps it had to go through to be created. Describe how it may have been put together by people working hard in a factory or shop. Make sure to start from the beginning of the process all the way through until it arrived at your house.

19. In most places, Labor Day is the final holiday before school begins. What are some of the things you and your family need to do to get ready for a new year at school? Do you enjoy gathering these supplies? Why or why not?

20. Several decades ago, it was much more difficult for women to get jobs than men. Why do you think it was so difficult for women to have a place available in the workforce? Do you think there is gender equality in the workforce today? Why or why not?

21. While Labor Day originally centered on workers' rights and labor unions, it is now more focused on vacations and enjoying time with family. Do you think this was a positive shift? Why or why not?

22. Work has transitioned in the last few hundred years from the fields, to the factories, and more recently to the computer. Do you think one type of work is more important than another? Why or why not?

23. Celebrating a day off of work when you don't have a job can be a difficult proposition. Imagine that you could create a job for a person who was unemployed. What would the job be and why?

24. While most people don't get a full-time job until after high school or college, many teenagers get part-time jobs to learn more about the working

world. What do you think your first part-time job will be, what might you learn from it, and why?

25. Knowledge of computers and the Internet is becoming more and more important for jobs. Why might it be difficult for a person who doesn't understand technology to get a job today? What new types of technology might people have to learn in the future?

26. The amount of jobs available in the country tends to fluctuate based on how well the economy is doing. What do you think are some things that make the economy better or worse? What would you do to change things for the better if you were in charge?

27. In the distant past, men and women worked under horrible labor conditions that led to long hours, injuries and even deaths. Labor laws and unions have made work a safer and better place. How do you think job conditions will continue to improve in the future and why?

28. Some people who work have their own businesses. If you could start any business what would it be and why? How successful do you think you'd be?

29. There are jobs that will be available after you graduate high school and college that don't even exist today. What do you think some of those jobs might be related to? Would you want one of the new positions? Why or why not?

30. How would the world be different if there were no unemployment and everybody had a job? What problems would it solve and what problems might it create? Would this be a better world? Why or why not?

31. What are some of the reasons that you would need to get a job? What are some of the things you might have to sacrifice in order to be able to work at the job and why?

32. When you go to a job interview, you often bring a list of all the successful things you've done to that point called a resume. What would go on your job resume right now? Do you think a potential employer would be impressed with your resume? Why or why not?

33. Imagine that you could create a job for yourself out of thin air. Someone would pay you to do exactly what you want to do for the rest of your life. What would you be doing at this job and why would you choose to do that?

34. While many full-time jobs now come with paid vacation and health insurance coverage, in the past employers gave workers little-to-no benefits other than a pay check. Why do you think companies didn't give their workers health coverage and other benefits? Why do you think that has changed in the modern world?

35. How much would you enjoy or not enjoy the following jobs: video game tester, astronaut, sports coach, gardener, and bike messenger? Explain why you would or wouldn't enjoy them.

36. What do you think would be the easiest job to do in the world and why? What would be the most difficult job in the world and why?

37. Do you think you'd enjoy having the same job as any members of your family? Why or why not? If not, do you think you'd be willing to do a job you didn't like to take care of your family?

38. What are some jobs that you think would make the lowest amount of money? Why do you think they earn the least? What are some jobs that would earn the highest? Why do you think they earn the most?

39. One job that earns a considerable salary is being a professional sports player. What do you think it would be like to be a pro athlete? What do you think your chances would be of making the big time and why?

40. You have been given the opportunity to try out five different jobs anywhere in the world. What jobs would you choose to test out and why? Which do you think you'd enjoy the most and why?

41. Some believe that Matthew Maguire, a machinist, was the first to come up with a holiday for workers that later turned into the first Labor Day celebration in 1882. Do you think someone at the bottom of a company could convince an entire nation that he and his co-workers deserved a holiday? Why or why not?

42. Others believe that Peter J. McGuire, a cofounder of the American Federation of Labor, came up with the holiday after seeing a similar celebration in Toronto, Canada. Have you ever been inspired after seeing someone do something cool? What was it and did you ever try to do it yourself? Why or why not?

43. Create a conversation between one of the two possible founders of Labor Day and his co-workers, discussing why there should be a holiday for workers. Does the co-worker agree with him? Why or why not?

44. New York City hosted the first celebration of Labor Day in 1882. Why do you think the Big Apple is the starting place for so many parades and festivals? Do you think a movement or holiday could start in your city? Why or why not?

45. A violent labor strike in Pullman, Illinois, in 1894 led to 13 deaths. Congress tried to reconcile by passing a law to make Labor Day a national holiday. Why do you think it sometimes takes something bad to happen before a law passes?

46. The initial proposal for the Labor Day holiday set out to create a public exhibition of the strength and togetherness of the labor organization. What are some examples of things a team of laborers may have created in your town? How could you express your appreciation for their hard work?

47. Labor unions have become less popular over the years as companies have paid more attention to the rights of workers. Why do you think companies have

made more an effort to treat workers more respectfully? How would you want to be treated if you worked a 9-to-5 job?

48. Imagine that you were marching with your family on the first official Labor Day in 1894. How would the holiday be different from the one celebrated today? Which would you enjoy better and why?

49. Teaching is said to be one of the toughest jobs out there. There are more than six million teachers working hard in the United States trying to educate their students. Imagine how hard it would be to be the teacher one of your classes. Do you think you would be able to handle the challenge? Why or why not?

50. Around the time of the original Labor Day, many people worked in factories. How different do you think your life would be if both of your parents worked long hours at a factory every single day? Do you think your parents would enjoy it? Why or why not?

ROSH HASHANAH

51. During Rosh Hashanah, honey is eaten to symbolize having a sweet new year. What do you think it means to have a sweet new year? What are some ways that you can have a year that is sweet?

52. Even though this holiday often falls in September, it is considered the Jewish new year because Judaism uses a calendar based on the moon. How do you think your life would be different if you used a different calendar than most other people?

53. To celebrate Rosh Hashanah, Jews gather in synagogues and listen to a musical instrument made out of a ram's horn called a shofar. What do you think a shofar might sound like? What do you think the blowing of the shofar might mean?

54. Imagine that you and your friends have been invited to a Jewish new year party even though you aren't Jewish. Describe what the party is like and what you and your friends do there for fun.

55. One tradition of Rosh Hashanah is for people to apologize to their friends and family for negative things they did to these people during the past year. If you wanted to apologize for the things you did wrong in the past 12 months, who would you apologize to and why? How would you feel after you apologized?

56. Imagine that your teacher or parent created a book with a record of who had good, bad, or average behavior in your class or home in the past year. Would you be labeled as good, bad, or average? Why? If you were bad or average, what could you do to move up to good?

57. Create a made-up story using the following words: apples, books, honey, and celebration.

58. Why do you think it's so hard sometimes to say you're sorry for something? Do you think that it will get easier or harder as you get older and why?

59. Many Jewish prayer services are conducted in the Hebrew language. Why do you think Jews don't conduct most of their service in English? How do you think you would follow along if you attended a service in a synagogue?

60. People of the Jewish religion have been treated badly by many different countries over the years. What do you think is the best way to avoid discrimination and mean acts against a religion or a race? What would you do if you saw someone making fun of someone's religion or heritage? Why?

COLUMBUS DAY

61. When Christopher Columbus first arrived at the Americas, he is believed to have thought he was in a completely different place on the other side of the world. Have you or your parents ever gotten lost like that? Where were you going and how did you find your way back?

62. In 1492, Columbus thought that he had landed in India and thought the people he spoke with were Indians. Who did he actually meet there? What do you think their reaction was to Columbus and his crew?

63. Imagine that you were the first to discover something either big or small. What would you discover and would people think your discovery was important? Why or why not?

64. Create a made-up story using the following words: map, ship, gold, and discovery.

65. Describe what you think the inside of Christopher Columbus's ships would have looked like. Use your imagination to go into as much detail as possible.

66. Imagine that you had to convince your parents to let you go on a great voyage with all of your friends. Where would the voyage lead you and how would you be able to gain permission for such a dangerous trip?

67. One of the reasons Columbus thought he had landed in India was that in the past people didn't realize how big the world actually was. What are some other things people in the late 1400s might not believe about how the world is today? Do you think they would like the discoveries that have been made since then?

68. Describe what you think the land looked like where Columbus first arrived in what is now called the Bahamas. Keep in mind that in 1492, the world was a much different place without nearly as many tall buildings and as much technology as we have today.

69. Some people in the time of Columbus used to think that the world was flat instead of being a sphere. How different would the world be if it actually were flat?

70. Columbus took four major voyages to the Americas, some of which took years at a time. How well do you think you could handle being on a ship in the middle of the ocean like that? What would you do to entertain yourself during the long trips?

71. Imagine that you have discovered a new continent! What would be the first thing you would do there and why? How would you get other people to believe you about your discovery?

72. Christopher Columbus bought orange seeds and the seeds of other citrus plant to the Americas from Spain. What are some things you would bring from your town to a foreign land? Do you think they would be as popular as orange trees? Why or why not?

73. Some states refuse to celebrate Columbus Day, making it a somewhat controversial national holiday. Why do you think Columbus Day is controversial? Do you personally think it should be celebrated? Why or why not?

74. Imagine that you and some friends are on a boat ride and that you are looking far off into the distance using a telescope. You see something surprising and you can't wait to tell everybody about it. What do you see and how will it change your life?

75. Being out at sea can be rough, especially for a person who gets seasick. Have you ever gotten seasick? If you did, how would you try to improve your condition?

76. If you had the opportunity to travel anywhere in the world via boat, where would it be and why? How long do you think the journey would take and what would you do when you arrived there?

77. How would the area around your hometown have been different in 1492? Describe what you might see if you went for a short walk through your town way back when.

78. As one of the first Europeans in the Americas, Christopher Columbus had the privilege of naming different places and things. If you were the first person in a new land, what would you name it and how would you name the plants and animals you saw there?

79. Imagine that you had to ask the President of the United States permission for a major project. What would the project be? How would you be able to convince him or her?

80. Create a dialogue between two members of Christopher Columbus's crew the day after they first spotted land in the Americas. What would the two of them have to talk about and why?

81. Imagine that you have discovered something completely new that nobody's ever seen before. What would the discovery be? How might you be treated differently? How would this new sighting change your life?

82. In the time of Columbus, being an explorer meant searching the seas for new trade partners, cultures, and colonies. What are some professions that focus on exploration today? How are they similar to Columbus and how are they different? Would you want an exploratory job? Why or why not?

83. You and your fellow villagers on the island of Hispaniola have spotted a ship off in the distance and none of you have ever seen anything like it. What do you and your peers think of the vessel? What do you think its intentions might be? How would you treat the crew members upon their arrival and why?

84. What would it be like to live off the land and use only what was necessary like the American Indians did at the time of Columbus? What are the benefits of such a lifestyle and what are the detriments?

85. Columbus took some natives home with him to Spain to prove his discovery. How would you feel if you were taken from your home to a new land with different clothes, a different language, and everybody staring at you? What would you do to cope with the situation and why?

86. Do you think it was fair for the Spanish and later the British and the Americans to take over land that was originally the home of the American Indians? Why or why not? How do you think your life would be different if the American Indians had been left alone?

87. Imagine that a new person your age has moved into your neighborhood. This person has toys, games, and an amazing house. Would you consider being this person's friend just to use all of the awesome stuff? Would you feel like you were exploiting this person? Why or why not?

88. While some look down on Columbus for his negative practices during the discovery process, others say that he was a product of his time. Which do you believe? Do you think that your actions today could be viewed differently 50, 100 or 200 years into the future? Why or why not?

89. The discovery of the Americas by Columbus opened up a Pandora's Box of new ships and new discoveries throughout North, South, and Central America. Imagine that you started a new trend that you couldn't stop. What might the trend be, how would it spread, and how would it make you feel?

90. You are the captain of the fastest space ship in the galaxy. You and your crew have spotted a new planet that not only seems inhabitable, but contains the first alien species the human race has ever seen! How will you proceed? What will you report back to Earth and why?

91. Festivals around the nation celebration Columbus Day with Italian food and entertainment, though it's never as large and wild as St. Patrick's Day for the

Irish culture. Do you think Columbus Day will ever become as big for Italians as St. Patrick's Day is for the Irish? Why or why not?

92. Some use the Italian leanings of the holiday to watch movies in Italian or with Italian characters. Describe a Columbus Day in which you immerse yourself completely in Italian culture. What do you do, what do you eat, and how do you enjoy it?

93. In Columbus, Kansas, pilots from all over the country fill the sky with colorful hot air balloons on Columbus Day. Do you think this event fits with the holiday? Why or why not?

94. Eastchester, New York, plays host to a homemade meatball and wine-making contest during Columbus Day. Imagine that you had to make all of your favorite foods from scratch at home for an entire month. What skills would you have to learn and how would everything turn out?

95. Miami hosts a three-day seafaring Columbus Day Regatta as sailors celebrate boating with parties and a trip to Key West. How do you think sailing has changed in the time since 1492? Would you rather go sailing then or now and why?

96. The annual New York City Columbus Day Parade often asks a prominent Italian-American to serve as its grand marshal. What do you think are the qualifications of a parade grand marshal? Who do you know that might qualify and why?

97. Columbus Day can also be a holiday to celebrate the practice of immigration, since most of our ancestors came to the United States from far away. How would your life be different if your long-ago relatives never made the trip to the U.S.?

98. Honoring American Indians is another Columbus Day staple, often by learning more about their heritage or visiting museums and presentations. Do you think it's important to hear both sides of a story? Why or why not?

99. The U.S. Virgin Islands and Puerto Rico celebrate Columbus Day as Friendship Day, a day of cultural exchange, food, and entertainment between the islands. What do you think is the importance of friendship between countries? Why is it important?

100. While Columbus was not the first to land on American soil via boat (the Vikings and other explorers have that distinction) he is the one celebrated for the achievement. Do you think that other explorers should also be celebrated during the holiday? Why do you think Columbus is the one who got the distinction?

101. Before Columbus Day was official, celebrations were held on the 300th and 400th anniversaries of Columbus's voyages, in 1792 and 1892. What are some things in your lifetime you might celebrate the several-hundredth anniversary? How do people remember an event from so long ago?

102. Columbus Day has been used as a day to support nationalism, war, and loyalty to the United States, even though Columbus came to the Americas long before the country was founded. Do you think Columbus thought that multiple countries would be created in the area he landed? Why or why not?

103. Columbus Day was first celebrated as a state holiday in 1906 in Colorado, though it was more like a St. Patrick's Day for Italian-Americans since Columbus was Italian. How do you think the holiday would be different today if it celebrated Italian heritage as opposed to the discovery of the Americas? Why?

104. Some initial attempts to make Columbus Day more national were opposed by businesses that didn't want to interrupt the busy fall season with another holiday. If you could have more holidays or fewer holidays, which would you choose and why?

105. One of the oldest continuous celebrations for Columbus Day takes place in San Francisco, which began celebrating in 1868. Imagine what it might have been like to be there for the first ceremony. How might it be different from the way the holiday is celebrated today?

106. Several cities and counties have replaced the holiday of Columbus Day with one called Indigenous People's Day. What do you think this name change means? Do you think the change will catch on over time or that people will always celebrate Columbus Day? Why?

107. In the last century or so, some opposition to Columbus Day has arisen because it seems that Columbus may not have been a very nice guy. Create a conversation between Columbus and one of the first natives he encountered on Hispaniola. Does Columbus seem friendly in the conversation or like more of a schemer?

108. Many natives grew sick after the arrival of Columbus and other Europeans because they didn't have immunity to European diseases. How different do you think doctors and healthcare were in 1492? What might natives and Europeans have used to try to heal themselves before hospitals and vaccines?

109. Multiple Native American organizations are not interested in celebrating a holiday like Columbus Day. Why do you think that is? Do you think it's important to hear both sides of a story? Why or why not?

110. There are multiple aspects of the Columbus Day holiday that don't seem worth celebrating, like slavery, disease, and a hostile takeover. What do you think should be celebrated about Columbus Day and why?

HALLOWEEN, VETERANS DAY AND THANKSGIVING

HALLOWEEN

111. Imagine that you are a piece of candy on Halloween. What kind of candy are you and how would you enjoy the holiday?

112. What is the spookiest thing you've ever seen on Halloween and why was it so frightening?

113. Write a made-up story using all of the following words: costume, candy, ghost, and pumpkin.

114. What do you want to go as for Halloween and why is it your costume of choice? Will your parents let you? Why or why not?

115. Imagine that every day on the entire calendar has now become Halloween, for 365 straight days of costumes, candy, and jack-o-lanterns! Would you enjoy so many chocolate-filled nights or would you just get a tummy ache? Why?

116. What kind of candy does your family give out on Halloween? Would you get them to give out something different if you had a choice? Why or why not?

117. What would be your perfect Halloween day and night? Describe everything from the moment you wake up to the end of the trick-or-treating session with your friends and family.

118. Describe the scariest Halloween costume or object you've ever seen. Why was it so terrifying? Do you think you could make something scarier yourself?

119. What might an actual ghost say about Halloween? Do you think he or she would enjoy it or think that the holiday is silly? How did you come to meet this chatty ghost?

120. Some people watch scary movies and television shows on Halloween. What do you think is the scariest movie or show ever? If you don't know any scary entertainment, you can make up your own film of fear and describe it here.

121. You've just walked into a huge Halloween costume shop filled with outfits and decorations from top to bottom. Describe the entire shop and the parts of it that appeal to you the most.

122. Imagine that you had the ability to carve a jack-o'-lantern into any shape you wanted. What kind of face or object would you carve into it? How would people react when they walked by when it was all lit up?

123. A spooky fog has started moving through your town on the morning of Halloween. Is it a ghost, or some strange type of weather? Where did it come from and what does it mean?

124. While Halloween is a ton of fun now, do you think you'll still want to dress up in a costume when you get older? Why or why not?

125. In a spooky turn of events, everyone in your class has turned into their costume! The princesses have become real princesses while the werewolves have become scary creatures of the night. What would you become and how would your classroom change?

126. Describe the creepiest, spookiest haunted house you can think of. What kind of scares might you experience from the beginning to the end of your tour?

127. Write a dialogue between a vampire and a werewolf. What might these two frightening creatures have to talk about and why?

128. What kinds of costumes do your family members tend to wear on Halloween? Who has the better costumes, you or them? Why?

129. As you and some friends walk by a scary graveyard, you spot a witch drinking a magic potion. Suddenly, the witch disappears and re-appears right next to you. What happens next?

130. Imagine that you have been given the chance to create your own candy for Halloween. What would you call it and what ingredients would go into it? Do you think other kids would like it?

131. One particularly scary Halloween activity is to be led on a ghost tour. Ghost tours involve tour guides taking groups to mysterious, haunted locations. Where in your area might a ghost town lead you? Would you be scared visiting such creepy places? Why or why not?

132. In Altoona, Pennsylvania, pumpkin farmers weigh their gargantuan pumpkins every fall, sometimes weighing pumpkins over 1,000 pounds! What would you do with a 1,000 pound pumpkin and why?

133. Imagine that you were placed in the middle of a Halloween corn maze that featured over a mile of paths. How would you and your friends find your way out? Do you think you'd enjoy the challenge of getting out? Why or why not?

134. In some Halloween traditions, families set out an extra place in honor of people who are missing but invited to be there in spirit. Imagine that a ghost your family knows actually came to dinner and sat down at the table! Who would the ghost be and what might you all talk about? Why did he or she decide to come?

135. In Damariscotta, Maine, each Halloween season residents compete in a pumpkin boat contest, carving a giant pumpkin into a boat and racing it through the water. Describe what it might be like to try to maneuver a giant pumpkin through the current. Why might it be difficult?

136. In Greenwich Village in New York City, participants create giant puppets like 20 foot long dancing skeletons and glowing caterpillars. Create a conversation between two of the giant puppets on Halloween. What might they think about the wild celebration and why?

137. In many foreign cultures, Halloween is taken less as a time for candy and more to remember ancestors. Who is your most memorable ancestor? Why has he or she made such a mark on your family?

138. While plenty of people decorate their houses for Halloween, a house certainly isn't the scariest building to begin with. What are some frightening buildings that would make really scary haunted houses and why?

139. Imagine that you have put together a Halloween costume party for pets! How might you dress up your pets and what are some examples of the animal costumes you might see? Would it be a success? Why or why not?

140. In some areas it is a Halloween tradition to visit the graves of famous people. If you could visit the grave of any famous individual, who would it be and why?

141. You have been diagnosed with allergies to chocolate, nuts, and other sweets. Your candy-eating days are over. How would the holiday of Halloween change for you? Would you still be interested in dressing up and playing games? Why or why not?

142. You have been chosen as the judge in a worldwide Halloween costume contest. People from around the world have submitted pictures of their elaborate disguises for you to pick from. What might some of the wildest entries be? How would you make your decision?

143. It's been 50 years since the space colony was established on a distant planet from Earth, and now that there are enough kids present, the first trick-or-treat in space has been approved. How will the holiday change now that it's millions of miles away? How will the costumes be different and why?

144. In a world where ghosts have been proven as real, now ghost children and human children go out trick-or-treating together. Describe a night going out on the town with a ghost family. How would the ghost kids enjoy the event?

145. You have been invited to a masked ball, in which you and your friends have to disguise yourselves so well, you won't be able to tell who you're dancing or speaking with. What costume would you choose? How well do you think you'd be able to guess who other people are and why?

146. What sort of things actually scare you? Why do you think they're so frightening?

147. You have become a pumpkin-carving artist, changing boring orange pumpkins into works of art throughout the fall season. What are some of your designs that are the most popular? How might you use your skills to help people in need?

148. Re-cast the scariest movie or television show you've ever seen with the members of your family. What part would each family member play and why? How would the movie or show change filled with the people you know the best?

149. After discovering a book of spells in the attic, you've found out that your family is filled with witches and wizards, including you! How would these new magical powers change your life? Do you think your Halloween nights would be different? Why or why not?

150. For Halloween, your parents have given you permission to eat candy for breakfast, lunch, and dinner. Which kinds of candy would you eat for each meal? Do you think you'd actually be able to make it through the day without any legitimate food? Why or why not?

151. During Halloween, many of us wear costumes that prevent other people from knowing who we are. What might be some reasons you would have to wear a disguise? How successful do you think you'd be at hiding your identity?

152. Create a conversation between two jack-o'-lanterns during the night of Halloween. What do they think of the holiday? Are they worried that they'll rot if they're left outside too long?

153. The night before Halloween is sometimes called "Mischief Night" and involves tricksters going around pulling pranks in their neighborhood. What are some examples of Mischief Night pranks? Why do you think these jokers think pulling pranks is funny?

154. Describe your group of friends in costume on the night of Halloween. Include what each person is wearing and the types of candy you're able to collect going door to door.

155. Imagine that your family has entered a Halloween house decoration contest. What spooky lights and objects might you put up in an effort to win? Would you win first prize? Why or why not?

156. You and your classmates are bobbing for apples in a giant tub of water. It's your turn and you clamp down on what you think is an apple and pull your head out of the water. Your classmates gasp – it's not an apple at all! What is it and what happens next?

157. Imagine you are sitting around a campfire with your friends and it's your turn to tell a scary ghost story. What story do you tell? Are your friends actually scared by it? Why or why not?

158. Create a song or poem about your ideal Halloween experience. Feel free to embellish with wild, somewhat-fictional details if you want.

159. In a last-second replacement, you have been hired as the director for a scary Halloween movie. What is the movie about? Who is starring in the flick? Does the public like your film? Why or why not?

160. Halloween has been going on in some form for over a thousand years. How do you think the holiday would have been different at its beginning? Would you rather celebrate the holiday in the past or in the modern day? Why?

VETERANS DAY

161. One difficult part of serving in the military is that soldiers often have to be away from their families, even during holidays. How do you think you would cope with being so far away from home? How would your family members express that they miss you?

162. Have you ever had any relatives who were involved with the military? What branch of the Armed Forces did they serve and did you ever see any pictures of them in their uniforms? What do you think the military was like for them?

163. Why do you think that it's important for veterans of the military to have a special holiday devoted to them? What are some ways in which you can show your appreciation for their service?

164. The American flag and the Pledge of Allegiance are two very important symbols of Veterans Day and the United States. Why do you think they're so important? What do you think it means when we salute the flag and say the pledge?

165. During some of the major wars like World War II and the Korean War, some animations studios made cartoons to support the war effort. Imagine that you were making a cartoon to support the troops. What would it be about and why?

166. Not all veterans are people who have fought in wars. Some work behind the scenes to improve the safety of the country in other ways. What are some ways in which you can help your country without fighting? Why do you think your help is important?

167. Create a made-up story using the following words: veteran, service, peace, and homecoming.

168. You and your friends have been asked to write a new song about America to honor the troops for Veterans Day. What kind of song do you write? What is the song about? Do you think that the veterans will enjoy it? Why or why not?

169. In the past, only men were allowed to serve in the military. Do you think it's important that both men and women serve in the military today? Why or why not? What are some ways in which we can honor the women who have devoted their lives to service?

170. If you had to pick among serving in the Army, Navy, Marines, Coast Guard, or Air Force, which would you pick and why?

171. What are some creative ways you can show support for a military serviceman? Which do you think he or she would like the best and why?

172. Create a conversation between two members of the Armed Forces who are stationed overseas during Veterans Day. What might they have to discuss and why?

173. Imagine that you are planning a party for a member of your family returning from military service. Who would you invite and what activities would you have available at the party?

174. The USO is an organization that boosts the morale of troops in part by sending entertainers all over the world to improve their spirits. If you were in the military, what entertainment would you want to see to keep your mood positive and why?

175. Imagine that you and your family have gone to one of the major monuments that honor military troops. Describe what it might look like and the different kinds of people you might see there. How do you think such a sight would make you feel?

176. Many soldiers are courageous in defending the nation and its people. What do you think it means to be courageous? Describe a time that you were courageous. What was it that made you display such courage?

177. In the past in the United States, people could be drafted into the military even if they didn't want to go. Do you think it's better that only volunteers go to the military now or do you think many people should be forced to serve? Why?

178. Imagine that you and your family have gone to volunteer at a veterans hospital. What would you do to help out the veterans at the facility? How might they express their appreciation for your help?

179. What do you think it means to serve your country? Other than military servicemen and women, who are some people who you think serve the country? Why?

180. What benefits do you think military servicemen should get when they return from active duty? Why do you think they deserve those benefits?

181. Hearing rousing speeches to honor the military is a frequent occurrence on Veterans Day. What do you think are some of the important elements of a Veterans Day speech? Who would be a good candidate to make such a speech and why?

182. It is a Veterans Day tradition to assemble care packages to send to military troops serving overseas. What do you think you would want to be sent to you in such a care package and why?

183. Veterans Day is known for amazing air shows in which military and civilian pilots show off their flying skills to the "oohs" and "ahhs" of the crowd. What do you think would be most difficult about being a pilot and why? Would you ever want to be a pilot? Why or why not?

184. In 2011, a new Veterans Day tradition came about in which a college basketball game was played on an aircraft carrier. What do you think it'd be like to play sports on the deck of a giant airbase in the middle of the ocean? What might be difficult about it and why?

185. One possibility for an activity on Veterans Day is visiting and listening to the story of an actual veteran. Imagine what it'd be like to hear his or her story. What might you learn about military service? How would such a tale affect you?

186. Two minutes of silence are frequently observed on Veterans Day to honor fallen troops. Do you think complete quiet is a proper way to show respect to military troops? Why or why not? If not, what alternatives might there be?

187. Veterans receive free food from many restaurants during the holiday, but what if you could cook for an entire household of veterans? What would you make for these honorable troops and why? Do you think they'd enjoy the occasion? Why or why not?

188. Wreaths are laid at the many different military memorials throughout the country on Veterans Day. Do you think memorials will change in the future as the world becomes more digital? Why or why not?

189. Some people take the time during Veterans Day to watch a movie about veterans to commemorate the holiday. Who would you most likely watch such a movie with in your household? What do you think you might learn from the film and why?

190. While military leaders have shown bravery during their service, they can have difficulty finding a job upon returning home. Do you think a veteran would make a good employee? Why or why not?

191. Imagine that you were a military hero returning from a brutal war. What would you expect your reception home to be like? How do you think all of the difficult things you saw during the war would affect you and why?

192. Becoming a part of the military requires some of the most intense physical and mental training in the world. Some describe the first stages of boot camp as the hardest thing they've ever done. Why do you think so many people are willing to go through such pain and hard work? Do you think a nearly impossible boot camp is necessary? Why or why not?

193. In the 1940s, superheroes like Captain America were depicted in comics as fighting alongside the military to try to win World War II. Come up with an idea for another American superhero who works with the U.S. military. What is his name, what are his super powers, and why does he fight for his country?

194. Upon going back to normal civilian life, some members of the military can have a difficult time readjusting. What do you think are some of the reasons a regular job and family life might be tough to slip back into? What might be some of the ways a service member could ease into that transition and why?

195. There are those who want nothing more than to serve in the military but can't due to an injury or a chronic condition like a weak heart. How might a person feel not being able to serve what was thought to be his or her purpose? What are some things these people could do to serve the American military cause without fighting?

196. The families of military service members have it tough as they have to hope and pray for the best for their brave family member. Imagine that you had to say goodbye to a close family member going away to the military. Where would you be, what would you say, and how would you feel?

197. It's late at night and your unit is far away from home in a remote village. You write a letter to your family about what you've been up to and how you miss all of them. Write that letter in great detail making sure to include all of your thoughts and feelings.

198. There are military members stationed in some of the most dangerous parts of the world. What might it be like to have to walk around in such a hazardous area? How would you feel and why?

199. How do you think the military and war in general will change over the next 100 years? As technology improves, will war get more brutal or will peace become more frequent and why?

200. The military is often dogged with reports of being unfair toward women. Why do you think it's difficult for the institution to treat women as equals and with respect? What would it take for women to gain more protection from assault and other incidents in the military? Why?

201. Veterans Day was originally called Armistice Day in a celebration of peace at the end of World War I. People hoped it would be "the war to end all wars," but that was not to be the case. Do you think universal peace is possible? Why or why not?

202. Raymond Weeks, a World War II veteran, is credited with starting the campaign to change Armistice Day to Veterans Day. Why do you think it's important to celebrate living veterans as well as deceased veterans?

203. During a very unpopular war called the Vietnam War, American soldiers were not honored and supported upon their return. Why do you think people turned their backs on Vietnam veterans? How do you think that made the veterans feel?

204. Imagine that you could take a veteran to school with you to talk to your classroom about his or her service. What might you all discuss? What do you think you might learn from the experience? Why?

205. One Veterans Day tradition is to pay respect to the multiple tombs of unknown soldiers in the United States, such as the one at Arlington National Cemetery. Do you think it's important to honor a soldier whose name has been forgotten? Why or why not?

206. What do you think it would be like to live in a world filled with peace? How would your day-to-day life change? Why?

207. Create a conversation between you and a relative who either served in a war or had friends who served in a war. What might this relative's opinion be about Veterans Day? How does it differ from your opinion? Why?

208. Many veterans are given free meals on Veterans Day. What else do you think veterans should be given for free during the holiday to honor their service? Why?

209. During Veterans Day, many parts of the world observe two minutes of silence to respect those who perished during World War I. Why might being completely quiet during that time be a good way to honor people? What would you think about during two minutes of silence?

210. Write a poem about what Veterans Day means to you and your family. Do you think a veteran would appreciate what you've written? Why or why not?

THANKSGIVING

211. Write a made-up story about Thanksgiving using the following words: turkey, family, football, and happiness.

212. What would happen if you got so full of food on Thanksgiving that you could hardly move? What would your family say?

213. After hearing the phone ring, you pick it up to talk to the person on the other line. Only, it's not a person calling at all, it's the Thanksgiving turkey! What does the turkey have to say and how do you respond?

214. Who is the most interesting person you've talked with at a Thanksgiving dinner? Was it a distant relative? A family friend? What made him or her so unique?

215. What is your favorite food to eat on Thanksgiving and why is it your top choice? What is your least favorite Thanksgiving food and why don't you like it?

216. You have gone back in time to the first Thanksgiving! How is the inaugural Thanksgiving different from the way your family celebrates the holiday?

217. How would your Thanksgiving feast be different if you had to cook all the food yourself? Who would you ask to help you and why?

218. What are you the most thankful for this year and why are you so grateful? What do you think your family members are the most thankful for?

219. At the first Thanksgiving, the American Indians helped the pilgrims to find and grow food for a feast. Who is someone who has helped you to do something? How did you thank this person for his or her help?

220. *Continue this story.* She opened the cupboards and let out a scream. You rushed over to help and looked. Someone had taken every last bit of food on Thanksgiving morning. The holiday was ruined, unless you could come up with a plan...

221. Have you ever helped your family cook the Thanksgiving dinner? If so, what kind of jobs did you have to help prepare the feast? If not, imagine how you would help create the various tasty dishes that line your Thanksgiving table.

222. Thanksgiving is renowned for its famous side dishes like mashed potatoes and broccoli casserole. What is the strangest side dish you've ever had at Thanksgiving? What made it so strange and how did it taste?

223. Imagine that you have been given the honor of offering up a toast or prayer at the beginning of the Thanksgiving meal. What will you say and how will your family react?

224. Write a conversation between a side dish and a main course at the table during turkey day. What do the two delicious plates have to discuss with one another?

225. The turkey carver of the house has given you and a friend a chance to break the wishbone in half. You successfully pull off the bigger pieces and get one wish that is bound to come true. What do you decide to wish for? Why?

226. After a light-hearted argument, one of your family members grabs a handful of food from his plate and tosses it across the table. Before long, it's a full-on family food fight! Describe the entire battle from beginning to end. Why did it begin and how does it end?

227. Describe all of the smells and sights of the Thanksgiving table. What do certain smells and sights make you think of as you're writing about them?

228. After a dream about Thanksgiving, you've woken up to discover that you've grown a layer of feathers like a turkey. What do you tell your parents? How will you deal with your bird-like situation?

229. Imagine that you and your family have decided to help out at a homeless shelter's soup kitchen on Thanksgiving morning. How do you feel about being able to give back to people who might have otherwise gone hungry? Does it make you appreciate your full Thanksgiving plate? Why or why not?

230. Why is the holiday of Thanksgiving special to you? Do you look forward to it every year? Why or why not?

231. Imagine that instead of sitting around letting food digest after the Thanksgiving meal, your family went on a wild adventure together. Where might you go, what might you do, and why?

232. What are some of the things your other family members might be thankful for on Thanksgiving? Who might have the most interesting "thank you" and why?

233. The days after Thanksgiving are well known for their leftovers. What do you think is the best use of your Thanksgiving leftovers and why?

234. While some families brave the massive shopping crowds on Black Friday, others spend time together at home. Would your family rather shop or hang out on Black Friday? What would you do or where would you shop and why?

235. In Southern California, an animal shelter holds a Thanksgiving dinner for turkeys! The turkeys eat their favorite foods at a decorated table and bond with other animals at the shelter. Describe how this event might unfold. Would you enjoy attending? Why or why not?

236. On the opposite side of turkey traditions, there is an event in Indiana in which competitors use a chain to toss a cooked turkey as far as they can. How well do you think you'd do in the event? Would you enjoy watching it? Why or why not?

237. Imagine that your family has decided to dispense with traditional Thanksgiving food to have an international Thanksgiving! All of the usual fare has been replaced with different kinds of ethnic food. What kinds of food would you want at this eclectic dinner and why?

238. What would your Thanksgiving dinner be like if all of your family members had to dress up in costumes? What costumes would your family members choose and why?

239. Imagine that you and the other relatives your age have been asked to put on a play describing the story of the first Thanksgiving celebration. Who would play what part? What would the story be? Would your family enjoy it? Why or why not?

240. Since many other cultures do not celebrate Thanksgiving, Americans who live in other countries have a difficult time finding everything they need for a proper Thanksgiving meal. Imagine that you and your friends have to find a turkey, the side dishes and decorations in a foreign nation. What obstacles might you run into and why?

241. In some countries, food is not nearly as plentiful as it is in the United States. Imagine going through a Thanksgiving holiday in the midst of a famine. Could the holiday still work without the massive piles of meat, side dishes, and dessert? Why or why not?

242. With most of your family on a diet, the Thanksgiving meal has become a much more sensible and healthy affair. In what ways would the meal be different? Would you still be able to enjoy this reduced-calorie feast and why?

243. Imagine you had to write a letter to everyone who helped you at all in the past year. Who would be some of the people you wrote to? How many letters might you write in total? Who would you give the most thanks to and why?

244. It's the post meal football game and everyone in your family is playing, even your grandparents! Describe the two teams, the positions your family members play and the game itself in great detail. Who would win and why?

245. You can pick three guests, living or deceased, famous or non-famous, to join your Thanksgiving meal. Who would they be and why?

246. Instead of cooking, your parents have decided to order-in all of your favorite take-out food as a sort of delivery feast! You have the choice of three restaurants. Which ones do you choose and why? How does the low-stress, oven-free meal work for your family?

247. As part of a school project, you need to visit the Thanksgiving meal of all of your classmates or friends. How might each meal be different? How might the people be different at each gathering? What would you learn about the holiday in general and why?

248. A turkey, a pilgrim, and an American Indian walk into a house. What are they doing there? Why are the three of them hanging out together?

249. It's all over the news: one out of a million turkeys has come down with a condition: singing turkey disease. And one of those turkeys is in your house! What kind of songs might this turkey sing? How would having a musically-inclined bird change your family's holiday?

250. What is on your typical Thanksgiving plate? Do you pack it to the brim with as much food as possible? Do you only fill it with your three favorite foods? Use all of your senses to describe the plate in great detail.

251. Sarah Josepha Hale, an American journalist, is credited with leading the cause to make Thanksgiving a national holiday. Imagine that Thanksgiving was still only celebrated by a few states. How would you campaign to make it a day of feasting and fun for everybody? Would it work? Why or why not?

252. It was said that the Native Americans helped the pilgrims grow beans, corn, and pumpkins that were eventually used in the Thanksgiving feast. Have you ever asked someone for much-needed help? Who was it and how did this person help you?

253. Describe what the Plymouth pilgrim's colony might have looked like after experiencing hard times through storm and droughts during their first few years. How do you think they were able to endure such hardships?

254. Why do you think it's important to give thanks to people on Thanksgiving and throughout the year? How does it make you feel when people say "thank you" to you? Why?

255. One of the tastiest parts of Thanksgiving is the use of the meal's leftovers for the entire week after the holiday. What kind of leftovers concoction might you come up with for a snack? How would it taste?

256. Who are all the family members you might see during the Thanksgiving holiday? Which one are you most looking forward to seeing and why?

257. Thanksgiving is a major sports day, with college basketball, football, hockey and more throughout the day on television. If you could watch any sport after your tasty meal, what would it be and why?

258. Imagine that you had to be on a special diet during turkey day and you'll only be able to eat a few of the delicious foods on the table. Which three main courses and sides might you choose and why?

259. In a humanitarian White House tradition, the President of the United States pardons at least one turkey each year, keeping him or her from being cooked. What do you think the peaceful life for that turkey will be like for the rest of his or her days? Why?

260. What is the best Thanksgiving dessert you've ever tasted? Why do you think it was so good? Do you think you'd ever be able to replicate that recipe yourself? Why or why not?

Bryan Cohen

HANUKKAH, CHRISTMAS AND KWANZAA

HANUKKAH

261. In the story of Hanukkah, a tiny amount of oil was able to keep the candles lit for eight whole days. Imagine you had something last a lot longer than you thought it would. What would it be and how might it last so long?

262. Popular foods on Hanukkah included fried potato pancakes called latkes and friend donuts called sufganiyot. Why do you think the Jews eat so many fried foods during the holiday? Would you enjoy that part of the Hanukkah menu or would you rather have healthier fare?

263. Imagine you received gifts for eight straight nights instead of one. Would you rather have the biggest gifts first or toward the end of the holiday? Why?

264. The Hebrew letters on the side of the dreidel, the four-sided spinning top, mean "A great miracle happened there." Have you ever witnessed something you'd call a miracle? If so, what was it and how did it affect you? If not, imagine you saw something miraculous and write about why it impressed you.

265. Hanukkah is also known as the festival of lights in part because of all the beautiful candle holders known as menorahs. Describe a richly decorated menorah filled with eight lighted candles. Make sure to detail how you feel about the design and the brightly shining lights.

266. Dreidel is a simple game that often uses chocolate coins called gelt instead of real money. How would the world be different if all money was made out of chocolate? Why might it be a tough society to live in?

267. The story of Hanukkah starts with a local King banning the religion of Judaism and destroying the Jewish holy temple. How would you feel if a powerful person tore down a building you deeply cared about? Why do you think the King was so mean?

268. One tradition of Hanukkah and all year round is for people to give money and time to charity, which is called Tzedakah in Hebrew. What charity would you most want to support and why?

269. Create a conversation between the two candles on the Hanukkah menorah. What might the two of them have to talk about? Are they scared at all about being lit? Why or why not?

270. Imagine that you and your friends have decided to go to a Hanukkah party and a Christmas party on the same night. What might be some of the differences between the two? Why do you think both holidays are important?

CHRISTMAS

271. How would your life be different if Rudolph the Red Nosed Reindeer was your best friend? What kind of adventures would the two of you go on?

272. Describe your ideal Christmas tree. What would the ornaments, lights, and gifts look like? How hard would it be to set up?

273. It's Christmas morning, and after hearing a noise, you've tiptoed downstairs to get a closer look. As you peer around the hallway, you come upon a major surprise! What is the surprise and how do you react to it?

274. What is your favorite Christmas song and why do you like it? What is your least favorite Christmas song and why do you dislike it? Have you ever had to sing these Christmas classics?

275. What would you do if your next-door neighbor was a real-live elf? What kinds of questions would you ask and how would he or she answer them?

276. How would Christmas be different if you lived in the desert? How would the holiday change if you lived in the rainforest? Underwater? How about in the North Pole itself?

277. Do you think that you are on the naughty or nice list this year and why? What are some ways in which you could be nicer to the people you care about?

278. What types of presents do you think your parents wanted when they were your age? Would you have enjoyed those toys as much as they did?

279. Imagine that you have the choice to make whatever foods you want for a family Christmas feast. What would be on your special menu? How do you think your family members would like their dining choices?

280. What are some of the smells you think of when you think about Christmas? What people, places, and things do those smells remind you of?

281. Would you ever consider giving one of your Christmas gifts to a kid less fortunate than you and your family? Why or why not?

282. Why do you think it is that so many places are closed for business on Christmas? What do you think might be some of the places that remain open?

283. Imagine that you and your family have set up the largest Christmas tree display in the entire world. How big would it be? What would people think when they come to see this massive evergreen?

284. Imagine that you had a conversation with an ornament on your Christmas tree. What stories might the ornament have to tell about you and your family? Would any of the ornament's stories surprise you? Why?

285. Describe a snowy Christmas morning both inside and outside your house. Make sure to include as many details as possible about the snow itself.

286. Imagine if Santa's reindeer could talk just like humans. Write down a possible dialogue between two of the reindeer before their long journey on Christmas Eve.

287. Write a real or made-up story about a trip to see Santa Claus at the local mall. What was the experience like and what are the things you'll remember the most about the experience?

288. You and your family have run out of wrapping paper and all the stores are closed! What do you use to wrap your presents? How do your friends and extended family members react upon seeing your last-second replacement paper?

289. There are so many amazing Christmas treats, like cookies and candy canes, that are perfect for sweet snacking. What is your favorite Christmas treat and why do you like it so much?

290. During a walk around the block, you have stumbled upon a bottomless bag of presents with an unlimited number of gifts inside. What will you do with this powerful sack? Why?

291. In some families, Christmas gifts are hidden throughout the house like a game of Hide and Seek. Imagine if your family tried this tradition out. Where would the good hiding places be and in which rooms would you find certain gifts?

292. What are some movies or television shows that remind you of Christmas? Do you think your family would consider making that entertainment a yearly tradition? Why or why not?

293. Create a conversation between yourself and a version of you from one year ago. What will you tell the past version of yourself about Christmas? What might the past you remember about what you wanted during the holiday and why?

294. What would your Christmas celebration be like if everyone from your entire extended family came over for the holiday? How many family members would there be? Who might you enjoy spending time with the most and why?

295. During a snowy Christmas day, you and your friends have set forth on an adventure throughout the town. What activities might you plan and what goals would you want to achieve during your journey?

296. Describe an ornament you might create to show your family what Christmas means to you. Make sure to include what the ornament is made out of, how you made it, and what it represents.

297. If you could give a gift to one non-family member who would it be and why? What would you give this person as a present? What would the person's reaction be?

298. In Austria, Santa Claus is thought to have an evil twin named Krampus who punishes all the kids who misbehave. What would happen if Santa and Krampus confronted each other on Christmas Eve and why?

299. On Christmas Eve in Norway, families hide brooms because of a superstition that evil spirits might take them to ride around on. What would you do if you saw an evil spirit riding a broom? Would you be afraid? Why or why not?

300. In Caracas, Venezuela, churchgoers go to morning mass the week before Christmas using roller skates. Imagine if everyone in your town used skates to get around the entirety of Christmas week. How would this change traffic and why?

301. All gift-giving on Christmas has been abolished and the holiday is now only about food, family, religion, and friendship. How would this change the holiday for you and your family? Why would the holiday be worse and why might it be better?

302. Imagine that Santa Claus has asked you to help him create a magical sidekick to help him deliver presents throughout the world. What would this partner of present-giving look like, how would he act, what would his name be, and why?

303. A giant snowstorm the week before Christmas has stranded your family at a hotel in the middle of the country. With all the stores closed and all your relatives far, far away, how would the holiday change? Would you still be able to have some fun in such strange circumstances? Why or why not?

304. Putting together a family holiday like Christmas can be tough work for your parents and relatives. Imagine that you were in charge of planning everything from the decorations to the meals. What might be the most difficult part? What would you enjoy and why?

305. Imagine that a family 500 years in the future has found a video recording of your family Christmas celebration. What might this future family think about the way you talk, act, and celebrate? How would the family of the future celebrate the holiday themselves?

306. What are some of the nicest things you've done all year that make you deserve a great set of presents for Christmas? Are you proud of these moments of kindness? Why or why not?

307. What are the naughtiest things you've done in the past year? Do you think this changes whether or not you should get presents? Why or why not? How can you improve your nice-to-naughty ratio next year?

308. A burglar has crept into your house on Christmas Eve, and with everybody asleep, the only people who can stop it are the magical ornaments on the Christmas tree. Write a story about the ornaments coming to life to save your presents and kicking the criminals to the curb.

309. After securing two tickets to the North Pole, you and a friend or family member of your choice have traveled all the way to Santa's workshop. You knock on the giant wooden door. What happens next?

310. How would the world be different if everyone took magical sleighs to school and work? Describe the view you might see in your aerial journey throughout the town.

311. Imagine that you have been given the task to decorate the Christmas tree exactly how you want. What ornaments, lights, and other decorations will you use? What would your family or friends think about your decorative style?

312. What is your opinion on the tradition of mistletoe and kissing? Do you think it's unfair, strange, fun, or something else entirely? Why?

313. Describe the most beautifully wrapped present you've ever seen. Detail every aspect of the outside of it, along with its weight and what you think is inside.

314. Several hundred years ago, Christmas as it's celebrated today didn't exist. Santa was even thought to have a flying horse instead of reindeer. What do you think changed the holiday into what it is today? Why?

315. Create a conversation between two neighboring houses that are covered in lights on Christmas Eve. How do the lights make them feel and are they excited about the upcoming holiday?

316. One of the big traditions of Christmas is the creation of a nativity scene. Describe the most memorable nativity scene you can think of. Why do you think that depiction in particular was the one that stuck with you?

317. The Christmas season is one of the biggest shopping periods of the entire year. Imagine that you won a contest to go on a Christmas shopping spree. What would you buy and why?

318. Imagine that three wise men knocked on your door and stayed with your family to eat dinner. What would the wise men and your family talk about? Where would these three brilliant wanderers be off to and why?

319. Create a Christmas song that details how you and your family celebrate Christmas. The song can be funny or serious and go to any tune you can think of.

320. You have been hired by one of the biggest greeting company in the world to come up with some funny Christmas card ideas. What are some of your ideas? Why do you think they're hilarious?

KWANZAA

321. Kwanzaa was established by Dr. Maulana Karenga as a holiday of African-American identity and community in 1966. Do you think it's important for a group of people to have a collective identity? Why or why not?

322. The holiday of Kwanzaa was established in part so that African-Americans could reconnect with their African roots. Do you know where in the world your family is originally from? If so, how do you think it has affected the way you've grown up? If not, why might it be important for you to find out?

323. Kwanzaa is centered around seven principles, known as the Nguzo Saba. Each of the seven days of Kwanzaa corresponds to a different principle: unity, self-determination, collective work and responsibility, cooperative economics, purpose, creativity, and faith. Which of these seven principles do you think is the most important and why?

324. In Swahili, Kwanzaa means "first fruits." In ancient times, a first fruits ceremony featured a king or chief tasting the first ripe crops during a season. Imagine if every meal in your house was like a first fruits ceremony. Who would be the first taster? Who would be the last to taste? Why?

325. Households celebrating Kwanzaa decorate their households with colorful African cloths, the colors black, red, and green, and a candle holder with seven candles, called a kinara. Describe what it might be like to be invited to the house of a friend who celebrates Kwanzaa. What might you enjoy about it and why would you like it?

326. Kwanzaa is celebrated right after Christmas, from December 26 through January 1. Why do you think the holiday was placed immediately following Christmas? How might some people celebrate both?

327. The flag of Kwanzaa is black, red, and green. The black signifies the people, the red their struggle and the green for the hope of the future. As racism continues to be a part of the world, what do you think it will take for the "struggle" aspect of Kwanzaa to come to an end? Do you think equality can be achieved? Why or why not?

328. Kwanzaa is also a holiday of art, song, and creativity. Create a song or a poem about your thoughts on Kwanzaa and why you appreciate certain aspects of the holiday.

329. Imagine that you celebrated Hanukkah, Christmas, and Kwanzaa all in the same year. Which would be more important, getting three times the gifts or learning more about all three holidays? Why?

330. Since the holiday has qualities relevant not just to African-Americans but Africans around the world, also called Pan-Africans, the holiday has gained followers outside of the United States. Since it is such a young holiday, how do you think Kwanzaa will change in the next 100 years? Why?

NEW YEAR'S EVE, MARTIN LUTHER KING, JR. DAY AND GROUNDHOG DAY

NEW YEAR'S EVE

331. One of the strangest part of New Year's Eve is that we all watch a giant ball drop at the top of a New York City building to ring in the new year. Does your family have any strange traditions for New Year's Eve or any holidays? How did those traditions begin?

332. A resolution is a goal that people set to try to achieve during the coming new year. Do you have any resolutions for this year? What will you have to do to make sure they happen?

333. How do you think you've changed in the past year? How do you think you'll change in the next year?

334. Describe the most exciting and loud New Year's Eve party that you can imagine. Make sure to include the people there, the decorations, and all of the fun activities.

335. What is the best thing that has happened to you in the past year? Why does it stick out as the top moment during an entire 365-day period? What is something that could top that moment in the coming year?

336. Write a made-up story using the following four words: Resolution, party, countdown, and friendship.

337. Imagine that your family is planning to stay up together to watch the new year begin at midnight, but your power goes out at 11 p.m. sharp! Instead of going to sleep, you decide to tell stories about the past year to each other. What stories do you tell? Does this story-telling beat watching TV? Why or why not?

338. Some people go travelling for a year or more at a time to explore the world. How do you think your town, friends, and school would change if you went away to travel for a whole year? Would it change for the better? Why or why not?

339. What is the latest you've ever stayed up? What are some of the things you did with your extra nighttime? Were you glad that you put off sleeping for so long? Why or why not?

340. Imagine that you are a giant cartoon balloon for a New Year's parade floating above tens of thousands of people cheering. What are some of the things you see and hear from your vantage point high above the city?

341. What is the most unexpected thing that happened to you in the past year? How and why did this event change you?

342. Every time zone throughout the world will celebrate the new year as soon as their clocks strike zero. Imagine that you somehow attended every single celebration. What would you learn about the world? Which one do you think would be the best and why?

343. You will spend many hours sleeping and going to school over the course of the next year, but what is the activity that you want to do the most in the coming year and why?

344. In New York City's Times Square, hundreds of thousands of people party deep into the night on New Year's Eve. Imagine if you had to clean up all of the trash they left behind. Who would help you and how would you most effectively get it spotless by the following morning?

345. Create a conversation between yourself now and a version of yourself from a year ago. What would you have to tell the "past" you? Would the younger you have anything to remind you?

346. There will be huge crowds of people at many New Year's Eve parties throughout the world. Do you enjoy being part of a crowd? Why or why not?

347. You've been invited to a big New Year's Eve blowout, and it's time to pick your party outfit. Would you wear something in your closet or go out and get something new? What would people think of your fashion choices and why?

348. What do you think would be the best view to see some colorful New Year's Eve fireworks? Who would you bring with you to this special place and why?

349. Imagine that you could go back in time one entire year with the chance to change every decision you've made. How would you do things differently and why?

350. Who is someone other than yourself that you want to have a good year? Why? How can you help this person directly to improve his or her year?

351. In Mobile, Alabama, the maker of the Moon Pie marshmallow sandwich creates a 55 pound, 45,000-calorie moon pie in honor of the new year. Describe how you and your friends might try to eat the massive pie.

352. You and your friends have been commissioned to pick what object your town will drop as part of New Year's Eve. What object would best symbolize your town and yourself as an item to drop from the tallest building in the area? Why would you choose that in particular?

353. In some traditional New Year's Eve celebrations, instead of just dropping an object, a person is safely dropped inside of it! Describe what it might be like to be dropped on New Year's Eve in front of thousands of screaming fans. Explain the event from beginning to end.

354. In Bangkok, Thailand, over 500,000 people hold hands to count down the last seconds until the new year. Do you think that many people would ever hold hands in your town? Why or why not?

355. You might eat a spicy doughnut during the German New Year's Eve, as practical jokes including filling doughnuts with mustard instead of jelly are common. What practical jokes might your family try to pull on New Year's Eve and why?

356. In Belgium, a popular New Year's Eve activity is watching a stand-up comedian make fun of the past year using jokes. What are a few jokes you might make about the previous year? Would your friends find the jokes funny? Why or why not?

357. Some celebrators in Estonia believe that eating more meals on New Year's Eve than usual will give them the strength of that many people the following year. How many meals do you think you could eat in one day? Do you think the superstition could be right? Why or why not?

358. In countries like Ireland and the Netherlands, smaller get-togethers are often favored over bigger parties. Would you rather have a giant party or a small gathering for New Year's Eve? Why?

359. In Turkey, New Year's Eve is connected with raising money for the poor. What charitable event might you want to raise money for at the end of the year? How would giving your time to charity make you feel and why?

360. You couldn't have a New Year's Eve celebration without fireworks! Why do you think fireworks are so popular? What is your personal opinion about watching fireworks? Would you rather do something else to ring in the new year? Why or why not?

361. Some people view the new year as a new beginning. What does it mean to have a new beginning? In what ways could you commemorate this fresh start and why?

362. While many people create New Year's resolutions like losing weight or earning more money, few are ever able to achieve them. Why are these resolutions so hard to keep? What are some ways to make goals easier to reach and why?

363. A lot can happen in a year. What are some of your predictions for the next year, both for yourself and for the world at large? What do you think will cause these changes?

364. How and why do you think the following people will change in the next 365 days: your best friend, your parents, your siblings, your teachers, and yourself?

365. You have come across a telescope that allows you to see exactly one year into the future. You can't interact with what you see but you are able to take

information from it. How would the view of one year forward change the way you live your life now and why?

366. What is the most important event coming up for you in the next year? Why? What might be the most important event for your friends and your parents? How could you help them during their event and how might they react as a result of your aid?

367. What are three things that happened in the past year that were completely unexpected? Why were they so unanticipated? What surprises might you have to look forward to next year?

368. Upon returning home, your parents tell you about a mysterious package that has arrived for you. It appears to be addressed from you, 10 years in the future. What is in the package? Why and how did the future version of you send it your way?

369. You have been chosen to give a New Year's Eve toast just before midnight to praise the previous year and discuss the bright future ahead of you and your friends. What would you say during the toast? How would your friends react and why?

370. Imagine that you were required to create a to-do list at the end of every year for the following year. What would you put on this mandatory list and why? Do you think you'd get everything on the list completed? Why or why not?

371. New Year's Eve is the final day of the Gregorian calendar, the calendar that most of the world uses. Some countries and religions use different calendars, so they have a celebration on a different day. What would it be like to use a different calendar with different months and holidays than most people?

372. In 1582, Pope Gregory XIII instituted the Gregorian calendar to fix an error in the previously used Julian calendar. Imagine if you found a mistake that required everyone to change something they used every single day. What might it be and why?

373. Many people take the final week of the year to remember what happened in the previous year. Would you rather look backward to what happened or look forward to the new things that are about to happen? Why?

374. One New Year's Eve tradition is to make a toast to the upcoming year. Which of your friends would you choose to make such a speech at your celebration? What would he or she talk about and why?

375. While most people think of Thanksgiving as a time to give thanks, some religious New Year's traditions involve giving thanks for all the great things that have happened in the last year. What are some of the best things that happened to you in the outgoing year? How could you best give thanks to the people responsible?

376. You can watch the ball drop in New York Times Square on New Year's Eve, but it isn't the only item dropped to ring in the new year. Oranges, beach balls, crabs, ducks, ukuleles and even reality TV stars have been dropped to signify the new year. What item do you think your town would enjoy dropping during the holiday and why?

377. The Polar Bear Club is a group of brave, crazy individuals who jump into the freezing cold water on New Year's Day, often to raise money for charity. Describe what it might be like to dive into such ice-cold water. How would you feel and would you ever do it again?

378. Babies born at the beginning of New Year's Day are sometimes given prizes that range from baby food to gift certificates for being a New Year baby. What do you think it would be like to have your birthday on New Year's Day every year? Would you enjoy it or rather that your birthday be on a less-celebrated day?

379. Auld Lang Syne, a poem published by Scottish poet Robert Burns, is often sung after the clock strikes midnight on New Year's Eve. The song is meant to remember the past year with fondness, even though some things will be forgotten. What things might you forget in the next year that you remember now? Why?

380. Many celebrants use noisemakers for fun on New Year's Eve, but originally it was thought that such noise would drive away evil spirits. Do you believe that loud noises keep us safe from ghosts and ghouls or that such things simply don't exist? Why do you feel that way?

MARTIN LUTHER KING, JR. DAY

381. Why do you think it's important for people to treat each other equally regardless of who they are and where they come from? Why do you think some people have a hard time doing that?

382. Imagine a situation in which you use peace and understanding instead of violence to deal with the problem. In what ways would your non-violent approach be more successful?

383. In some areas, Martin Luther King, Jr. Day is a day of service. What are some ways that you could serve your community? Why might you choose these methods of service above some others?

384. Have you ever noticed any discrimination against you or one of your friends? If so, how did the discrimination make you feel? If not, write a story about seeing discrimination and how you would react to it.

385. Create a made-up story using the following words: race, color, speech, and equality.

386. Imagine that you had a dream of how the world could be a better place? What are some of the things that might happen in that dream? What are some ways in which you could make the dream actually happen?

387. When Dr. King was alive, people would listen to his speeches on the radio and feel happy and inspired. Who are some people that we watch on TV or online who make us feel the same way today? Do any of your friends inspire you? If so, why?

388. What do you think it means for all people to be treated equally? What are some ways today in which some people are not treated as equals? Why do you think there is still inequality in the world?

389. Why do you think name-calling is a mean thing to do? Why do you think some people do it even when it hurts other people's feelings?

390. Imagine that you had to give a speech to more than 25,000 people about the state of the world today. What do you think you'd talk about? Would your speech be a success? Why or why not?

391. Why do you think it's important for people to have equal rights regardless of race, color, or belief? Why is it difficult for certain people to believe in equal rights?

392. At one time, Dr. King was able to rally 200,000 people to peacefully march for civil rights. What are some causes today that could peacefully get so many people to come together? Where might such a rally occur and why?

393. Imagine that you were in a place where people didn't treat you well because of how you looked or what you believed. How might you feel and why would you feel that way?

394. Dr. King had a dream for a better world. How do you imagine the world will become better during your lifetime and why?

395. What does it mean to "do the right thing?" Why do you think some people choose to do the easy thing as opposed to the right thing?

396. One message that Dr. King preached was peace, even when people are being mean to you. How hard would it be to keep your cool when other people are calling you names? Why do you think Dr. King felt that being peaceful was a better response than fighting back?

397. Describe a conversation between Dr. King and yourself. What questions would you ask him and what would you learn?

398. Why do you think segregation is wrong? How would you try to convince someone in support of segregation that it was not fair? Would you be successful? Why or why not?

399. Describe what the scene may have looked like in Washington, D.C., when tens of thousands of people gathered for Dr. King's "I Have a Dream Speech." Make sure to include how people reacted to the words he spoke.

400. What would you use your powers of speech for if you were as strong an orator as Dr. King? What subjects would you speak about and how would you use your speaking powers for a good cause?

401. There are many museums and tours one can take on Martin Luther King, Jr. Day to learn more about African-American history and civil rights. What is one aspect of the subject you'd like to learn more about and why?

402. Over 100,000 people take the time to volunteer during the holiday. What do you think it means to have a day of service as opposed to a simple vacation day? Why might a day of service be important?

403. Peaceful marches and demonstrations happen all over the country during Martin Luther King, Jr. Day. If you could hold a demonstration for any good cause what would it be and why?

404. One example of a holiday activity is holding a roundtable discussion with your friends or classmates about the importance of civil rights. Imagine that Martin Luther King, Jr. himself was involved in the discussion. Describe the conversation from beginning to end.

405. In Denver, Colorado, the city holds a Martin Luther King Marade, a combination of the words march and parade. What are some example of strange two-word combinations you could make? Why might they be confusing to some people?

406. Many people take time during the holiday to watch television specials about Dr. King and his contributions. Do you think watching these documentaries and programs is important? Why or why not?

407. During the civil rights movement, Dr. King hosted spiritually-based dinners meant to have people discuss the barriers that remain to progress. What would such a dinner be like in your household? What would you discuss and why?

408. The city of Hiroshima, Japan, is one of the few outside of the United States that celebrates Martin Luther King, Jr. Day. What do you think it would take for the world to recognize the holiday as strongly as the U.S. does? Why?

409. One way that Dr. King's memory has been honored is by naming many street, libraries, and schools after the civil rights leader. What opinion do you think Dr. King would have of these honors and why?

410. While Dr. King's work made a lot of progress for civil rights, there are still many issues that need to be resolved for true equality to exist. What are some causes Dr. King's supporters might be fighting for today and why?

411. While it is important to be able to speak out on what you believe in, it can be a dangerous practice if you're discussing a controversial issue. Do you think it's still worth it to try to right injustice? Why or why not?

412. Dr. King found an issue he believed in, equality, and he devoted his life to the cause. What is something that you strongly believe in? Do you think you'd ever be willing to talk to millions of people about it? Why or why not?

413. Multiple aspects of civil rights that Dr. King was peacefully fighting for have come true. How do you think he would feel after seeing these practices come to pass? Why?

414. What parts of everyday life would Dr. King still be fighting to change if he were alive and well today? Why would he continue the cause when so much has already been achieved?

415. Imagine that Dr. King knew that he was going to be assassinated approximately 24 hours before it happened. Do you think he still would have continued to speak? Would he have done something differently to wrap up his life? Why?

416. How do you think the modern age of technology has changed the way that people can speak about what they believe in? Has it changed for the better or the worse and why?

417. Imagine that you had a family member with a completely different belief from you. How would the two of you peacefully resolve the issue? Why might it be better to use kindness instead of anger to deal with the conflict?

418. While Dr. King talked about non-violent methods of dealing with inequality, other speakers at the time, like Malcolm X, were more willing to resort to violence. Why do you think other speakers weren't willing to go along with Dr. King on a more peaceful path? What issues might come up in using violence that wouldn't result from using compassion? Why?

419. Do you think equality is important in areas like the workplace, marriage, and in education? Why or why not?

420. Who are some book, television, and movie characters that remind you of Dr. Martin Luther King, Jr.? What are some ways in which they are similar and what are ways in which they are different? Who would you rather have on your side in a conflict and why?

421. Martin Luther King, Jr. was assassinated in Memphis in 1968 after giving a speech to black street repairmen who were on strike after being mistreated. While Dr. King couldn't have known the end was near, do you think he would've been happy to know he spent his last day continuing the civil rights mission? Why or why not?

422. Even though Dr. King preached non-violence, his assassination led to riots in more than 100 cities. Why do you think people went against his message after he was gone? Was there anything that could have persuaded those who loved King to stay peaceful? Why or why not?

423. In a eulogy that Dr. King wrote himself, he asked that no mention of his honors and awards be made but that people talk about the things he tried his best to do. Would you rather people talked about things you've won and your trophies or the ways in which you've helped people? Why?

424. While Michigan Congressman John Conyers, Jr. proposed a law to make Dr. King's birthday a holiday in 1969, it took nearly eight years for Congress to vote on it. Imagine what it'd be like if you asked your parents for something and you had to wait eight years for them to make a decision. What might you have asked and why would they wait so long?

425. Over three million people signed a petition to make Dr. King's birthday a national holiday. Why do you think so many people supported making it a holiday? Why might some not support it?

426. Coretta Scott King, Dr. King's widow, spoke in front of Congress before their vote in 1979. Would you ever suggest that someone you know deserves a holiday? If so, who would it be and why? If not, do you think you'd ever deserve a special day to honor yourself? Why or why not?

427. Congress initially rejected the bill by five votes, stating that the United States had never given a holiday to a person who hadn't served in the government. Imagine that you had to break a long-standing tradition to do what was right. What might the tradition be and why would you have to do something different?

428. A major push for the holiday was made by singer Stevie Wonder upon releasing a song about Dr. King called "Happy Birthday." Create a song that someone might write about you. Who would write it and what kind of song would it be?

429. The holiday still faced difficulty, with one Senator coming up with a 300-page document of the bad things King was connected with during his lifetime. How might you feel if someone wrote 300 pages about why you shouldn't get something? Who might do such a thing and why?

430. The bill was signed into law in 1983 and was first observed by all 50 states in the year 2000. How might Dr. King react to such news? What would he hope could result from his holiday reaching national status and why?

GROUNDHOG DAY

431. Imagine that you were counted upon to determine if spring would come early or not. What kind of media attention would you get? Why might people think you have such weather-predicted prowess?

432. Create a conversation between the famous Punxsutawney Phil and one of his groundhog brothers. What would their opinions be about Groundhog Day? Do they enjoy it? Why or why not?

433. Describe the inside of a groundhog's underground house. What sort of items might you find down there? Do you think it would be comfortable for humans? Why or why not?

434. Which prediction would you rather the groundhog make, six more weeks of winter or an early spring, and why?

435. If a weather-predicting groundhog sees his shadow, he almost immediately runs back into his burrow. What do you usually think when you see your shadow and why? How would your life be different if you were afraid of your shadow?

436. In the 1993 movie *Groundhog Day*, the main character relives the same day over and over again. Imagine that you were stuck in the same day repeated many, many times. What would you do with your time and why?

437. Have you ever made a prediction about whether or not something would come true? If so, were you right and why did you make the prediction in the first place? If not, predict something that might happen at some point in February. Why do you think that might happen?

438. You hear a whisper and look behind you. It's your shadow asking for your help. What does your shadow ask you to do and how are you able to try to save the day?

439. Imagine that the other woodland animals got jealous of Punxsutawney Phil and did everything they could to replace him. Would they be successful? Why or why not?

440. What if Punxsutawney Phil accidentally predicted six more *years* of winter? How would you cope with all the snow and ice? How would you get Phil to change his prediction?

VALENTINE'S DAY, WASHINGTON'S BIRTHDAY (PRESIDENTS WEEKEND) AND PURIM

VALENTINE'S DAY

441. What are some of the sights and sounds that come to mind when you think of Valentine's Day? What sights and sounds make the holiday different from regular days?

442. Imagine that you have to do a big favor for a friend by dressing up in a giant heart costume for a candy shop on Valentine's Day. How do people who walk by treat you? What do you get in return for this hearty favor?

443. What is the best valentine you've ever received and why did you like it so much? What is the best valentine you've ever given and what made it so special?

444. Valentine's Day is a holiday about expressing love to the people who are the most important to you. Who are the people you love the most in the world? Why?

445. What is the most memorable chocolate you've eaten in your lifetime? How did you come to receive such an amazing dessert? Describe how it tasted in great detail.

446. *Continue the story.* You opened up the envelope at your desk to count the number of valentines you received. Despite there only being 20 people in your class, you've counted over 100 valentines in total! You look up and notice that everybody is smiling in your direction...

447. Why do you think red and pink are the most common colors on Valentine's Day? How would you feel if you had to dress up in a bright pink and red outfit all day on February 14th? Why would you feel that way?

448. An alien has landed in your classroom on Valentine's Day and you have been given the task of explaining exactly what the holiday means. How do you explain this loving day to a little green man? Are there any parts of the holiday that confuse him? Why?

449. On Valentine's Day, many couples try their best to be romantic by going out to dinner and getting expensive gifts. What would you do to be romantic if you were in a relationship? Why do you think those things would be romantic?

450. You have been transported 100 years in the future to a digital and futuristic Valentine's Day! How would the holiday be different in the future? What would be some of the things you'd miss about the present-day love fest?

451. Cupid has invited you along on Valentine's Day to shoot some love arrows into unsuspecting men and women. Describe your day of spreading love and happiness from beginning to end.

452. What is the most romantic love story that you've ever heard? If you've never heard any romantic stories, make one up. Why do you think the story is so romantic?

453. Some people don't like the idea of being romantic. Are you one of those people? Why or why not?

454. Create a conversation between the chocolates inside a red-heart shaped box. What do these various shapes and sizes of candy have to talk about and why?

455. What do you think the secret might be to lasting love in a relationship? Is it candy and presents, or something harder to explain? Why?

456. You and your friends have opened a bag of conversation candy hearts to find that the messages are all wrong. They aren't about love or Valentine's Day at all! What are some of the things the candy hearts say? How do you think they got so mixed up?

457. What do you think is more important: love or money? Why do you believe that?

458. Write the craziest and silliest love poem that you can think of. It doesn't matter if it rhymes, just make sure it's completely goofy.

459. Imagine that you have been hired as a flower delivery person for Valentine's Day. It's your job to give surprise flowers to people on this special day. What are some of the reactions you get from these very excited people?

460. Describe a delicious Valentine's Day cupcake from the multi-colored frosting all the way through to the moist center. Make sure to describe how it tastes.

461. Imagine that you have taken a Valentine's Day tour of a chocolate factory. What are some of the free samples you might eat? What would you learn about the making of chocolate? Do you think you'd enjoy it? Why or why not?

462. Some people give hand-made coupons to their loved ones for chores, meals and more. What would be the best personalized coupon you could get from your loved ones and why?

463. Imagine that you have been sent on a scavenger hunt to find out who your secret admirer is. Where might the hunt lead you? Would the admirer be who you think it is? Why or why not?

464. A very nice thing to do on Valentine's Day is to hide notes for your loved ones to find during the day at work or school. What might the notes to your family members say? Would they appreciate them? Why or why not?

465. In Guatemala, Valentine's Day is about both love and friendship. Why do you think there isn't a friendship day in the United States? If there was, who would you celebrate with and why?

466. A German Valentine's Day includes the placing of a giant, heart-shaped gingerbread cookie around the neck of a loved one like a medal. What other dessert might you enjoy having hung around your neck and why?

467. Some nationalists in India dislike the commercial aspects of Valentine's Day and may burn greeting cards in protest. Imagine if you had to celebrate Valentine's Day with your family in secret. How might the holiday be different? How would the meaning of the day change?

468. One destination to spend Valentine's Day is Verona, Italy, the setting for the play *Romeo and Juliet*. Tours are set up to trace the steps of the tragic literary lovers. What literary characters might you want to go on a tour for? Where would you have to go and what might you see?

469. Describe your ideal Valentine's Day from the notes from your loved ones to the best chocolate from anywhere in the world. How might such a perfect pink holiday make you feel and why?

470. People who have no one to share Valentine's Day with often treat themselves to candy, movies, and a trip to the spa. Imagine that you have planned out a day just for yourself. What activities might it include and how would it be different from spending the day with others?

471. Do you think that love is an important part of life? Why or why not? Why might it be tough for someone to be happy without experiencing love?

472. Imagine that you are going on your first date some time during high school or college. Where would the date occur, what activities would you do during it, and would the person like you enough to go on a second date?

473. One of the most mysterious and exciting things on Valentine's Day is to receive a note from a secret admirer. Do you think you'd ever send a valentine without including your name? Why or why not?

474. Imagine that one of your friends has just received a secret admirer letter and has asked you to help him or her to find out who it is. What are some of the ways you'd try to narrow down the suspects? Would you be able to identify the admirer by the end of Valentine's Day? Why or why not?

475. If someone wanted to be your valentine, what would be the best gift the person could get you and why? How do you think you'd react if this potential valentine gave you the exact gift you wanted?

476. What is the most romantic love story you've ever heard? Why do you think it was so romantic? Would you want something like that to happen to you when you're older? Why or why not?

477. While shopping for valentines, you stumble into a back room filled with love potions and love spell books. Would you buy and use any of these magical items? Why or why not?

478. You wake up one morning and find that everything in the world has turned pink for Valentine's Day! How would this change your typical day? Would you enjoy this pink existence or dislike it and why?

479. What do you think it means to fall in love with someone? Do you think that you'll ever fall in love yourself? Why or why not?

480. When two people are in love, they can act pretty silly with pet names, weirdly high-pitched voices, and a lot of staring off into space. Do you think that you'll act like that when you fall in love? If so, why? If not, how will love affect you differently?

481. The ancient Romans celebrated the feast of Lupercalia, a precursor to Valentine's Day, but it was a very different day indeed. Activities included drinking, sacrificing of goats and hitting people. Why do you think the Romans celebrated such a strange holiday?

482. Valentine's Day merged with Lupercalia and eventually with a more romantic holiday called Galatin's Day. Imagine that you could combine several different holidays together. Which ones would you choose and why?

483. The holiday didn't become associated with romance until the author Geoffrey Chaucer connected the holiday with love in a poem. Imagine that you had the power to change the way something worked just by writing it in a poem. What would you want to change and why?

484. Paper valentines have been discovered from as far back as the late 1400s. Describe what you think a nearly 600-year-old valentine might look like. How would it look different from the valentines used today?

485. One of the first poems to state that "roses are red and violets are blue" was written by Edmund Spenser in 1590. Create a poem using that famous line that ends in a surprising way.

486. Factory-made valentines began circulating in England in the early 19th century and eventually spread to the United States. What do you think it was that made these cards so popular for people to send to one another? Have such cards lost their value in a time of e-mail and technology? Why or why not?

487. These valentines were nearly all handwritten with notes and poems. What kind of note might you want to write to someone you really care about and why?

488. Now Hallmark makes millions of dollars selling valentines during a very commercialized holiday. Do you think that valentines should be more personal or that it's OK to buy cards that are mass-produced? Why do you feel that way?

489. Along with the cards, many give their loved ones chocolate and other gifts on Valentine's Day. What kind of gift would you want from a loved one for the holiday? Why?

490. Some people without a significant other on Valentine's Day refer to the holiday as Single Awareness Day. What do you think the term "single awareness day" means and why would people want to celebrate it?

WASHINGTON'S BIRTHDAY (PRESIDENTS WEEKEND)

491. Imagine that you were holding a birthday party for the President of the United States. What kind of foods might you serve and who would you invite to this huge event?

492. What do you think are some of the toughest responsibilities for the president of a country? Do you think it's the kind of job that you or your friends would be able to handle? Why or why not?

493. Imagine that you grew up in the time of George Washington and John Adams. How do you think your everyday life would change? What are some of the things you might miss and why?

494. Of all the former Presidents of the United States that you know, who do you think is your favorite and why? Who is your least favorite and why?

495. Since George Washington isn't still around to receive gifts, what do you think are some special things you could do to honor the first U.S. President on this holiday? Do you think he would appreciate your efforts? Why or why not?

496. Create a made-up story using the following words: honor, independence, president, and service.

497. George Washington was a very capable leader, helping the United States to gain independence and to start off the U.S. government on the right foot. Have you ever had to be the leader in a group or situation? Do you think you were a strong leader? Why or why not?

498. Washington's birthday is the day to honor many soldiers who have received medals for their military service. Have you ever received an award for doing something important? If so, what was it for and how did your family react? If not, what is a reward you would like to receive and why?

499. Imagine that you and your class had to put on a historical play about any time period of your choosing. What time period would you choose and which of your classmates would play certain figures throughout history? Why would they fit those roles in particular?

500. It's been said that George Washington and other people of his time wore wigs and had wooden teeth! Imagine what the world would be like if your teachers, family, and friends also wore wigs and used wooden teeth. What kind of wig might you get for yourself and why?

501. There are many stories about George Washington that may or may not be true. Imagine that someone came up with a tale about you that was completely

made up. What would the story be about and would people believe it? Why or why not?

502. One legend of George Washington is that he refused to lie to his father about cutting down the family cherry tree. Do you think you would tell the truth if you accidentally broke your parents' property? Why or why not?

503. After the Revolutionary War, George Washington could have been elected King of the United States if he'd wanted. Why did he decide not to take such a powerful position? Would you have made the same decision and why?

504. Imagine that you had to pay extra and unfair taxes for the things you liked the most, like the colonists had to pay to the British. How would you make your voice heard that the taxes were wrong?

505. Create a conversation between two troops during the Revolutionary War talking about their general, the soon-to-be president George Washington. Do they like working with him? Why or why not?

506. How do you think you could handle having to sail and march through the middle of the winter like Washington's army? What would you do to stay warm and how would you stay motivated to keep moving?

507. When Washington was elected as the first President, he received more than 50 percent of the votes from every single state. No President has ever done that since. Why do you think he was so popular? Will there ever be such a unanimous vote again?

508. Who are some other people you'd consider putting on the one-dollar bill? Why would they be an equally strong choice as a monetary portrait?

509. Would you ever want to be President of the United States? What might some of the challenges be? What would be the things you'd enjoy about the position?

510. Who are some other Presidents that you think should have their birthdays celebrated? Why are their lives important enough to be celebrated?

511. One way to celebrate Washington's Birthday is to visit or take part in re-enactments of the Revolutionary War. What opinion do you think actual soldiers from the 1700s might have about these re-enactments and why?

512. There are many historic sites related to George Washington that could easily be visited or read about on this important day. What places from George Washington's life might you want to visit and why?

513. In Laredo, Texas, residents celebrate Washington's Birthday for an entire month with concerts, colonial proms, food, and more. What other holidays could you see celebrating for an entire month? How would those holidays change and why?

514. To tie in with the story of the cherry tree, Alexandria, Virginia, restaurants take part in a Cherry Challenge to create the best cherry foods and

drinks. Describe what your ideal cherry-filled three-course meal might be. How often would you eat such a meal and why?

515. Imagine that you could have tea with Martha Washington, Ben Franklin, Thomas Jefferson, or others who knew George Washington personally. What would you discuss? Would they surprise you with any of their never-before-told stories and why?

516. For over 100 years, Eustis, Florida has been host to the George Fest, an annual event filled with food and fun. If you were the George Fest organizer, what events and activities would you include to celebrate Washington's Birthday? Why?

517. Mount Vernon hosts a cooking competition in which chefs fight to make Washington's favorite breakfast, hoecakes swimming in honey and butter. What is your favorite morning meal? What would it be like if several chefs tried to perfect your breakfast every day?

518. On Washington's Birthday, the U.S. Senate annually reads Washington's farewell address from when he voluntarily left the office of the presidency. Write your farewell address about all of your accomplishments and your hopes for the future.

519. In some states, Washington's Birthday is combined with the celebration of other Presidents, war heroes and civil rights activists. Who would you combine the celebration of Washington with if you had a choice and why?

520. George Washington's birthplace in Popes Creek, Virginia, has become a national monument and a place for celebration during his birthday. Imagine that your birthplace became a national museum about you. What exhibits and items might be shown there? What would a tour guide of your life talk about and why?

521. George Washington was one of the most important founders of the United States. Imagine that you and some friends created something and that you were appointed the leader. What would you all create, how were you selected as leader, and what will you do in that role? Why would it succeed or not succeed?

522. At many times in the Revolutionary War and the first few years as the President, Washington did what was best for the nation as opposed to himself. Have you ever done something that was good for the team instead of yourself? If so, what was it and why did you do it? If not, imagine you have and detail other people's reactions.

523. Imagine that George Washington was born in this day and age. Would he still be a politician or would he work in another profession? How would he use his leadership skills and charisma in the modern world and why?

524. Do you think that George Washington was the best President the United States has ever had? Why or why not? What qualities would have made him better at his job and why?

525. You have decided to run for the presidency of the United States...in the year 1800. How might the campaign process be different back then when compared to today? Without the Internet, television, and radio, how would you spread the word about your platform? Would you win? Why or why not?

526. George Washington became famous because of his strong leadership during a time that absolutely craved it. Nowadays, one can become famous from a wild online video or being a reality television star. Which type of fame would you rather have and why? How might each type of fame be different?

527. What do you think George Washington's friends thought about him during the war and while he was President? What sort of nicknames might they have called him? What pranks might they pull on him when he was least expecting them? How would they view George the regular guy?

528. You have taken control of George Washington's life for one day during either the Revolutionary War or during his presidency. What do you do, how does it feel and what new things might you learn about how people view him? Would you enjoy your out-of-body experience? Why or why not?

529. What other Presidents do you feel deserve some credit on Washington's Birthday? Do you think that each of the Presidents should have a holiday? Why or why not?

530. George Washington has had a state, a capitol, and plenty of towns and people named after him. What would it be like to have your namesake all over the place? Would you be proud? Would you let it go to your head? Why would you deserve it?

531. Washington's Birthday was actually celebrated as a sort of holiday by the French Army while Washington was still alive during the Revolutionary War in 1781. Imagine that people you didn't even know were celebrating your birthday. What might they do to commemorate the occasion and why?

532. Washington's 100th birthday was celebrated in 1832, and the Washington Monument's cornerstone was laid in 1848. Would you want a monument to be created in your honor? Why or why not? If so, what would you want it to look like?

533. The official federal holiday of Washington's Birthday was put into practice in 1879. Create a conversation between two kids, one who is excited about the new holiday and one who doesn't know who Washington was. How would the excited kid explain why Washington was important?

534. There has been some confusion over Washington's birthday because he was born on February 11 using the old Julian calendar and February 22 in the current Gregorian calendar. Imagine that you had your family convinced that you had two distinct birthdays. Would you be able to get presents on both? Why or why not?

535. In the 1930s, near what would have been Washington's 200th birthday, his face was carved into Mount Rushmore. Imagine what it would be like if your town featured a giant picture of your face. What would your friends and family think? How would your enlarged features make you feel?

536. Washington's Birthday and other holidays were moved to Mondays in 1971, in part so that people could have three-day weekends. Are you glad the Monday Holiday Act gave everybody a chance for three straight days off? Why or why not?

537. When the holidays were moved to Mondays, some people felt like they lost their meaning. For example, because of its placement on the third Monday in February, Washington's birthday would never be celebrated on Washington's actual birthday. Do you agree that the holiday loses some of its meaning? Why or why not?

538. In 1976, Washington was promoted to the rank of six-star General of the Armies so that he would continue to be the top commander even long after he was gone. What do you think it would be like to be the commander of the entire Armed Forces? Would you be a successful leader? Why or why not?

539. While some states refer to the holiday as Presidents Day, it's still technically called Washington's Birthday at the federal level. Do you think you'd rather have a holiday honoring Washington alone or all the presidents at the same time? Why?

540. Washington's Birthday is often used as part of a three-day Presidents' Weekend sale. Which do you think is more important: having discounted cars and other items or honoring George Washington? Why might both be important?

PURIM

541. Purim is a Jewish holiday that celebrates the escape from a plot by an evil advisor to the King of Syria who recommended all the Jews be killed. Imagine that you overheard an evil plan and you were the only one who could stop it. What would you do and why?

542. The story of the holiday begins with a Jewish woman named Esther winning a beauty contest to become the new queen of the nation. Do you think it's important to consider more things than looks when deciding on a partner? Why or why not?

543. Esther's cousin Mordecai finds out about a plot to kill the King, and after saving the ruler's life, he is rewarded with a parade. Imagine that you have found out a major secret. What could the secret be and what would you do with that knowledge?

544. The villain of the Purim story, Haman, is booed and hissed at when his name is mentioned during the reading of the tale. Do you think it's important to know the story behind a holiday? Why or why not?

545. Haman's hat is used as the model for the Purim pastry treat known as the Hamantaschen, which is filled with fruit, chocolate, or another filling. Imagine that you were to create a dessert based on some random objects. What would the things be and what would you end up creating?

546. One Purim tradition is a masquerade ball in which masks are worn throughout an entertaining party. What kind of mask might you wear to such an event? Would people have trouble recognizing you? Why or why not?

547. Mishloach manot, which means sending food gifts to friends, is a major tradition of Purim. Which of your friends or family members would appreciate a care package of their favorite foods? What foods would you include and why?

548. Charity giving is also important on Purim, which includes the distribution of food and money to the poor. Do you think it's important to contribute to people without a lot of money or possessions? Why or why not?

549. Esther displayed bravery by approaching her husband the king in an effort to save her people. Have you ever felt responsible for someone else or a group of people? If so, what did you have to do to support them? If not, how might you deal with that responsibility?

550. Reading the story of Purim from the Book of Esther is a major tradition during the holiday. What is your favorite story to tell and why?

INTERNATIONAL WOMEN'S DAY, ST. PATRICK'S DAY AND APRIL FOOLS DAY

INTERNATIONAL WOMEN'S DAY

551. Create a made-up story using all of the following words: women, respect, equal, and achievement.

552. Describe a famous woman from history using your imagination. Guess how you think she would look and act based on what you know about her.

553. It took the United States over 100 years to grant women the right to vote. Why do you think it was so difficult for men to give power and rights to women? Why do you think women deserve those rights?

554. Who is the greatest female role model in your life? Why is she so important to you? How would you react if you met her?

555. There are many places in the world that continue to deny basic rights to women, such as school. What do you think it would be like for a woman to grow up there? Why do you believe these places continue to be unfair toward women?

556. Have you ever heard any stories about growing up from your mother or grandmother? If so, how were their experiences different from how a girl would live today? If not, create a story about either your mother or grandmother using your imagination.

557. Imagine that you weren't allowed to do things that the other gender could. You couldn't go to the same classes or play with the same toys, etc. How would that make you feel?

558. Write a letter to a famous woman alive today congratulating her on her success. Make sure to include how her achievements have impacted you. Ask your teacher how you can send it directly to the woman in question.

559. In the past, women weren't allowed to play nearly as many sports as men. Why do you think it's important for men and women both to be allowed to play sports?

560. What are some ways in which you can honor the important women in your life on International Women's Day?

561. How do you show appreciation to the women in your life? What are some ways in which you can be more respectful and kind, particularly on this international holiday?

562. Why do you think it's important for women to have equal education throughout the world? Why might some people in power want to withhold education from women?

563. In some parts of the world, women are forced into marriages at a very young age and are punished if they refuse. Why do you think it's important for a woman to be able to marry who she wants?

564. There are many important women inventors, artists, and business creators in the world, but they are often overshadowed by male accomplishments. Why are women's achievements sometimes ignored or disregarded?

565. Imagine that you have been sent several hundred years in the past to observe how differently women were treated. What are some things you might notice? How has the world changed in its views toward women since then?

566. Sexism is when one gender is treated unfairly or like the inferior gender. What are some ways in which you've noticed sexism toward men or women? Why do you think sexism still exists?

567. International Men's Day is November 19, but it doesn't seem to get as much attention as the women's version of the holiday. Why do you think that is? What things might be celebrated on International Men's Day?

568. Create a conversation between a grandmother and granddaughter discussing how women's rights have changed in the last 50 years. How would the granddaughter feel about some of her elder's stories? Why?

569. How can boys and men help to stop gender inequality? What are some reasons they might be interested in helping out?

570. Imagine that you were not allowed to remove a head covering even on the hottest days of the year. How would that make you feel? Why might you not enjoy it?

571. International Women's Day is not typically celebrated in the United States. What do you think a celebration of the holiday would be like in your town if the holiday were as big as Mother's Day? What might your family do in honor of the occasion? Why?

572. In one International Women's Day campaign, women stand on bridges between two connected countries in a demonstration of peace. What do you think these bridges symbolize? Why might such a campaign get attention?

573. Some people use International Women's Day as an opportunity to make a small loan to women in need throughout the world. What might be some reasons that women need $20 to $30 in developing countries? Would you ever consider donating? Why or why not?

574. In some areas of the world, women use the holiday as a protest day in an attempt to get equal rights and pay. Describe what you think such a protest might look like. Could you ever see the women in your life going to such an event? Why or why not?

575. In South and Central Asia, events are held to bring attention to abuse, forced marriage, and a lack of education among women. What do you think can

be done to show more support for women in these parts of the world? Why might there be resistance?

576. In parts of Africa, female soccer players visit areas of the continent that do not have gender equality when it comes to sports. What are some reasons that men and women should be allowed to play sports equally? Why are athletics important for empowerment?

577. Throughout Europe, events are held to honor the most inspirational women in the world. Who is the most inspirational woman you know? How would you explain why this woman should be honored?

578. Another set of events for International Women's Day centers on art created by female artists. Describe what it might be like to attend an event filled with art created by women. How might you be affected by it?

579. Throughout the world, many companies give away gifts like free cupcakes, movie tickets, and flowers to all interested women during the holiday. Some women are resistant to these gifts. Why might they resist accepting such presents?

580. Imagine that you were to hold an event for women from every country in the world in your backyard. What would the theme of the event be? What activities would you have available and why?

581. There are parts of the world in which women are treated badly from a young age. International Women's Day is meant, in part, to try to help these girls and women. What do you think are the best ways to help and why?

582. Some of these girls are told that they will never amount to anything and that they aren't allowed to go to school. What are some reasons that it is a bad idea to be so negative about a person's future? What would you tell this negative person if you had a chance and why?

583. In these underdeveloped parts of the world, there are more restrictions placed on women than there are on men. Why do you think it might be unfair to keep girls and women from being able to do things that men can? How might the countries suffer from imposing these restrictions?

584. There are high levels of male-on-female abuse in these areas and there aren't nearly as many laws as in the United States to protect these women. Imagine that you were a politician in one of these areas and could propose a law to help. What would the law be and how would it help women?

585. While female abuse is higher in some parts of the world, it is still much too high in the United States as well. Why do you think some men have a difficult time respecting women the way they should be? Why is it important to teach that respect from a young age?

586. Imagine that you have started an organization to help women start their own businesses throughout the world. What might some of those businesses be?

How would you help them to get on their feet? What might the end result of your efforts be and why?

587. There are many ways that men joke with or about women that can be mean and nasty toward females. In what ways might these types of jokes make women feel negatively about themselves? What would be a better way to treat women and why?

588. How would the planet be different if it were flipped and men were being treated as inferior throughout the world? Would that be any more fair of a situation? Why or why not?

589. Who are some of the most inspirational women you've ever heard of? What kinds of lessons might these successful women be able to teach to young girls and why?

590. How do you think the situation of international women's rights will change in the next 100 to 1,000 years? What steps forward might the initiative take and why? How will these changes affect the world at large?

591. One of the precursors to International Women's Day was celebrated in the United States after women garment workers protested against poor working conditions. Why might a boss not treat his female (or male) workers with respect?

592. During such early women's strikes, both men and women in the area apparently made fun of women demanding better conditions. Why do you think people mocked the women instead of joining them?

593. Create a conversation between two women in the early 1900s hoping for equal treatment in the workplace and the home. How do you think the two of them would be encouraged by how the world has changed since that time?

594. In those early days, women and children alike were forced to work much more than 40-hour work weeks with little to no pay. Imagine that you had to work in sweat shop instead of going to school. How would your typical day be different? Why would it be unfair?

595. The first International Women's Day in 1911 saw men and women alike arguing for women's rights to voting, equal pay and equal treatment at the workplace. How would you feel if you weren't given the same rights as your friends and family members? In what ways might you protest your lack of equality?

596. Early feminist activists like Mother Jones and Elizabeth Gurley Flynn were often arrested or mocked for their desire to improve women's rights. Why do you think it has become more accepted nowadays for women to speak out against unfair treatment?

597. International Women's Day wasn't officially recognized until 1977, after a United Nations declaration. Why do you think it took more than 60 years from the first celebration for the holiday to be made official?

598. In many countries, women still don't have equal access to education, training, science and technology. Do you think it's important for women to get equality all over the world? Why or why not?

599. Write a poem about the most inspirational woman in your life. Make sure to include why she inspires you and how she has impacted your life.

600. Why do you think International Women's Day has not caught on in the United States as much as it has internationally? If you could host a celebration for women in the U.S., what would it consist of and why?

ST. PATRICK'S DAY

601. Imagine that one day you sat down to lunch like usual and found yourself across the table from a leprechaun! What does the tiny, green man tell you about his life, Ireland, and all his gold?

602. Have you ever seen a four-leaf clover? What would you do if you found this lucky plant? How do you think your life would change?

603. St. Patrick is partly famous for a myth in which he drove all the snakes out of Ireland. Have you ever had an experience with a snake? Would you keep one as a pet? Why or why not?

604. What would you do if you found a pot of gold at the end of a rainbow? Would you use it yourself or give some of it away to charity and why would you make that decision?

605. You and your family have won a free trip to Ireland! How do you think Ireland would be different from your home country? Do you think they would celebrate St. Patrick's Day differently? Why or why not?

606. St. Patrick's Day is all about the color green. Describe the greenest outfit you can think of from your forest green hat all the way down to your emerald shoes.

607. Create a made-up story using the following word: Irish, clover, green, and family.

608. Imagine that you were the luckiest person on the face of the planet. How would you use your luck to help yourself and to help other people? How would people treat you differently?

609. What is the greenest place you've ever been? Describe some of the plants and animals that set such a green scene. How often would you visit this place if you had a choice? Why?

610. St. Patrick had a holiday named for him, but what if someone named a holiday for you? How would people celebrate such an important day? Why?

611. Imagine that you have decided to visit a St. Patrick's Day parade wearing a "Kiss Me I'm Irish" T-shirt. How do you think people would react? Why might you wear a shirt like that?

612. You have been recruited to play in an Irish bagpipe band. How long do you think it would take you to learn the instrument and what would your friends and family think about your new talent?

613. Create a conversation between two Leprechauns on St. Patrick's Day. What might these tiny creatures talk about and why?

614. Dancing is a major part of Irish heritage. How do you think your family would change if all of you went out dancing more often? What kinds of dances do you enjoy doing?

615. In honor of St. Patrick's Day, some cities turn their rivers and other bodies of water completely green! How do you think they make the water green and why?

616. On St. Patrick's Day, lots of people drinking green beverages and eat green food. What is the greenest meal you can think of, from appetizer to dessert? Would you enjoy this emerald-style eating?

617. You and your friends have set off on a hunt for a four-leaf clover to improve your luck. Why do you need the extra luck and where do you go to look? If you found it, how would you use the luck to your advantage?

618. In Ireland, the Blarney Stone is a piece of a castle that is kissed by thousands of tourists a year to unlock hidden powers of intelligent speech and humor. What would you do if you gained such powers? Would it be worth kissing a piece of rock to do it? Why or why not?

619. Since Leprechauns are known for causing mischief, some people set up traps to catch them. How would you go about catching the small, green-wearing creatures? What would you do with them if you got them and why?

620. The harp was one of the most famous instruments in ancient Ireland. Imagine that you have attended a harp concert. Describe the sounds of the angelic instrument. Do you think you'd enjoy listening to harps playing all the time? Why or why not?

621. The world's shortest St. Patrick's Day parade is held in Hot Springs, Arkansas, and is only 98 feet long. What is something you've experienced that was much shorter than the norm? In what way was it short and how did you feel about it?

622. The Arkansas parade also features the Irish Order of Elvi, a group of Irish Elvis impersonators. Imagine that your favorite musicians pretended to be extra Irish. How would they be different? Would you still enjoy their music? Why or why not?

623. Montserrat, an island in the Caribbean Sea, celebrates St. Patrick's Day because a portion of the inhabitants descended from Irish Catholic settlers. What holidays might you celebrate if you were honoring your family's heritage from hundreds of years ago? What would those holidays mean to you?

624. Imagine that you and your friends have been commissioned to create a float for your town's St. Patrick's Day parade. What will the float look like and why? Will you win the first prize of a trip to Ireland? Why or why not?

625. During St. Patrick's Day celebrations in New Orleans, people pass out beads and decorations as well as potatoes and cabbages. What would you do if someone gave you a sack of potatoes and cabbages in the middle of a parade? Why?

626. While drinking is a part of many St. Patrick's Day festivals, in Manchester, England, celebrators begin drinking two full weeks before the holiday begins! How much work do you think adults actually do during that time? Why do you think they start partying so early?

627. One St. Patty's parade in the 1970s was labeled one of the shortest and worst of all time, featuring a green-painted cow, some dogs, and a goat. Describe what you think the worst St. Patrick's Day Parade would include? Do you think it'd still be fun? Why or why not?

628. In St. Paul, Minnesota, the parade for St. Patrick's Day crowns Miss Shamrock and Mr. Pat, the queen and king of the festivities. Imagine that you have been named the king or queen of the parade. What would it be like to be the center of attention and why?

629. In many cities, an Irish Catholic mass is held for churchgoers. Have you ever been a religious service you were unfamiliar with? If so, what was it like and why? If not, imagine that you have and describe how you might feel about it.

630. Imagine that you've woken up on St. Patrick's Day speaking not English, but Gaelic, one of the official languages of Ireland. What will you do when your family can't understand you? How will this change your St. Patrick's Day experience?

631. St. Patrick's Day is a holiday meant to celebrate Irish heritage. Do you think it's important to celebrate your own heritage? Why or why not?

632. If you were to have a festival for your own heritage, what kind of activities would you take part in? What colors and costumes might you wear? What would you eat to commemorate your ancestry and why?

633. Irish cultural heritage is loud and clear on St. Patrick's Day, but what about on other days of the year? What are some other aspects of Irish culture that you experience during the rest of the year?

634. There are many different cultures that have mixed with American culture other than simply Irish culture. What are some other cultures that you notice in

your everyday life including your food, music, language and more? Why do you think America has become such a melting pot of different cultures?

635. What are the benefits of having a society that includes multiple cultural influences? What issues might come up if Americans tried to resist all other cultures and remain completely American in every way? Why?

636. As different cultures adapt to the modern world, how do you think cultural influence will change in the next 100 years? Will different countries act more similarly? Why or why not?

637. On St. Patrick's Day, the color green makes you think of Ireland, leprechauns, and clovers. What does the color green make you think of on other days? Why might a person dressed all in green on a non-St. Patrick's Day come across as strange?

638. Imagine that you woke up on St. Patrick's Day with completely green skin! How would your family and friends react? What might be the benefits of your St. Patrick's Day-tinted outer layer? How would you try to reverse whatever changed you into shamrock color?

639. Many adults use cultural holidays like St. Patrick's Day and Cinco de Mayo to drink a lot of beer and get crazy. What aspects of the holidays might these crazy partiers miss out on? Why might being wild and uninhibited be more important to them than Irish culture?

640. St. Patrick, the namesake of the holiday, has visited your family for dinner. As a very religious man, what might he have to say about what St. Patrick's Day has become? Do you think there would be any aspects of the holiday he would like? Why or why not?

641. St. Patrick, who was originally born in Britain, was taken to Ireland as a slave. Eventually, he would end up teaching values throughout the country and becoming a national hero. How do you think St. Patrick was able to forgive the Irish for taking him away from his home? Why did he choose to be nice to them after what they did?

642. At first, the color connected with St. Patrick was actually blue. Imagine that famous holiday figures such Santa Claus were connected with totally different and strange colors. How do you think the holidays would change and why?

643. Legend has it that St. Patrick used the three-leaf shamrock to teach the Irish about religion. What are some other items found in nature that could be used to teach people lessons? Would they work as well as a book or a computer? Why or why not?

644. While Ireland celebrated St. Patrick's Day as a religious holiday, it became more about Irish culture when it was celebrated in the United States. Why do you think the holiday became more cultural?

645. What do you think St. Patrick, a very religious man, would think about all of the drinking, food, and games that go along with the holiday connected to his name? Write a letter from him, addressed from beyond the grave to the United States, asking for some changes to be made to this raucous, green celebration.

646. The first St. Patrick's Day parade occurred in New York City in 1762, when soldiers with the English army marched through the streets. How do you think the St. Patrick's Day parade has changed in over 300 years since that first march? Which one was probably more fun and why?

647. While Ireland made St. Patrick's Day an official holiday in 1903, in the 1990s, it decided to make it wholeheartedly Irish. The festival now includes Irish folk music, theatre festivals and fireworks that promote Irish heritage. Describe what it might be like to take part in such a festival in the heart of the Irish nation.

648. A famous St. Patrick's Day and Irish meal is the combination of corned beef and cabbage. Imagine that you cooked this holiday meal for your family. Do you think they would enjoy it? Why or why not?

649. St. Patrick's Day celebrations occur all over the world, including Argentina, Canada, Great Britain, Japan, New Zealand and more. Which country's celebration might you want to visit next year and why?

650. In 2012, Guinness World Records named St. Patrick's Day as The Friendliest Day of the Year, with over 400,000 people celebrating worldwide. What makes St. Patrick's Day so friendly? What days might be even friendlier than the Irish holiday and why?

APRIL FOOLS DAY

651. Have you ever had someone pull a prank on you? What was the prank and what was your reaction to it?

652. What do you think it means to be a fool? Have you ever acted like a fool yourself? What are some foolish things you've done?

653. Imagine that someone in town has pulled such a wild and crazy prank that it's affected the entire school. What is this massive prank and how did the person pull it off?

654. Some pranks for April Fools can be found online, such as fake news headlines that seem real. List or make up three Internet pranks and the people you know who might be fooled by them. Why are these people so easily tricked?

655. April Fools Day can be fun, but sometimes pranks can be mean instead of fun. Why do you think some people make jokes and tricks that hurt other people's feelings?

656. Create a made-up story using the following words: prank, laugh, joke, and confusion.

657. Describe the inside of a practice joke shop that contains every kind of prank you can imagine. Make sure to go into detail about the sights, sounds, and smells.

658. Imagine what kinds of pranks the following people would pull on April Fools Day: a magician, a billionaire, a firefighter, and your grandfather.

659. What are some ways in which April Fools Day might be different now than it was 50 years ago? How might it be different 50 years in the future?

660. After a full day of joking, it's probably best to be extra nice to your friends and family to make up for all the pranks. How would you go about being nice and apologizing to the people you just pranked?

PASSOVER, EASTER, EARTH DAY AND ARBOR DAY

PASSOVER

661. Passover is a Jewish holiday that celebrates the Jews' liberation from slavery in Egypt. Imagine that you were forced to build the ancient pyramids with your friends and family. Would you want to keep working or mount an escape? Why?

662. Imagine that your family grew up under the rule of a tyrant in a foreign land. How different would your life be today? What are the things you'd miss the most about your current life and why?

663. One of the ways that the Jews celebrate Passover is with a meal called the seder. The meal includes several strange foods like bitter herbs, multiple Hebrew prayers, and the story of the holiday. Describe what you think a seder might look like. How might you feel if you were invited to one but unfamiliar with the traditions?

664. Originally, Passover may have been more deeply connected with bringing an animal sacrifice to a holy temple than a family meal. Why do you think animal sacrifice was such a big deal in ancient times?

665. When the Jews asked the Pharaoh of Egypt for freedom, he stubbornly refused to let them leave. Do you know anyone who is stubborn all the time? Why do you think it's hard for some people to be flexible?

666. According to the Torah, God tried to sway the Pharaoh by unleashing a series of 10 plagues on the Egyptians, each one worst than the previous one. Create a conversation between two Egyptian guards witnessing both Pharaoh's stubbornness and the plagues of frogs, locusts, blood water and more. What would their opinion be about letting the Jews free?

667. The final plague is where Passover gets its name. The Torah says that God told the Jews to place the blood of an animal on their doorsteps and instructed the angel of death to "pass over" the marked houses, while slaying the firstborn child in the Egyptian houses. Why do you think this scary final plague finally convinced Pharaoh to let the Jews go?

668. As the story goes, the Jews were in such a hurry to escape Egypt, they didn't have time to let their bread rise. As a result, they ended up with unleavened bread called matzo. Imagine that you planned to cook or create something and ended up with something completely different. What would you do with it and why?

669. As a tradition of Passover, Jews remember their escape from Egypt by eating only foods that are unleavened, most of which are made from matzo. What

do you think it would be like to have to eat special food for eight straight days? What are some bready favorites you might miss the most?

670. One of the songs sung on Passover is called Deyenu, which roughly means "it would have been enough." It's about how the Jewish people would have been happy with one miracle but ended up with many. Have you ever gotten an unexpected bonus? How did it make you feel and why?

EASTER

671. What is the best treat you could ever hope to find in an Easter egg? How excited would you be if you actually found it and what would you do with such a prize? What would make the treat so special?

672. You hear a knock on your front door and it's the Easter Bunny! He says that he's extremely tired and could use some motivation to keep delivering Easter baskets around the world. What do you say to the Easter Bunny to give him the pep talk he needs?

673. Describe the most colorful Easter egg you've ever seen. What are all the different colors represented and how would you describe the pretty pattern if there is one?

674. Imagine that the animal of Easter was not a bunny at all but some other animal entirely. What animal would you choose to be the face of the holiday and why? What are some of the other ways the holiday would change with this new and improved animal?

675. Easter is one of the biggest holidays of the spring season. What is the thing you like the most about spring and why? What is the thing you like the least about spring and why don't you like it?

676. It's a tradition for people to try to wear some of their finest clothing on Easter for Church services. What do you think your Easter outfit would look like if you were trying to look your best? How would you try to spice it up to make it more interesting and why?

677. What kind of candies and toys would make up your perfect Easter basket? Why would you choose those items specifically?

678. Create a made-up story using the following words: bunny, egg, bonnet, and sunshine.

679. You and three of your friends have gained entry into a worldwide Easter egg hunt with a big cash prize! Describe the hunt from beginning to end, including whether or not your team is the winner.

680. While Easter is full of candy eggs and decorative eggs, sometimes the best kind of egg is one you cook. What is the tastiest kind of egg you've ever had

and why was it so good? What are some other foods that have eggs in them that you enjoy?

681. Easter comes at the end of the Christian period of fasting known as Lent, in which people give up certain types of luxuries or habits for 40 days. What are some things and activities that you think you'd have a hard time giving up for 40 days? Which would be the toughest and why?

682. Create a conversation between two marshmallow Peeps on Easter. Do they enjoy how popular they've become? Are they scared of being eaten? Why or why not?

683. Imagine that you and your friends have signed up for an Easter egg-rolling contest. The first to the end of the course with the egg still in their spoon wins. Which of your friends would win and why?

684. Who in your family would most enjoy the practice of painting an Easter egg? Why do you think that family member is the most artistic?

685. Americans eat billions of jellybeans during Easter. What is your favorite jellybean flavor and why?

686. Describe a beautiful Easter basket filled with candy. Detail everything inside, from the green paper grass to all of the delicious treats.

687. Somehow you've become stuck inside a chocolate Easter egg! What will you do to escape? How might you have gotten in there in the first place?

688. Imagine that you and your family have been transported into a cartoon world. Your next-door neighbors are a bunch of talking baby chicks and a human-sized Easter bunny! What are some of the other strange things you see in this animated world? Do you enjoy living there? Why or why not?

689. Even though Easter is a very important religious holiday, it has become one of the biggest candy-eating days of the year. Why do you think candy became such a major part of the celebration?

690. Imagine that one of your pets began laying candy Easter eggs. People from all over the world have come to see your magical animal. What happens next and why?

691. In Washington, D.C., it is an Easter tradition for children to roll eggs on the White House lawn. What might it be like to hang out with the President and other politicians during the Easter holiday? What questions might you ask them and why?

692. Sweden's Easter tradition involves children dressing up as good witches and trading cards and letters for candy and eggs. Create a conversation between a good witch and an evil witch on Easter. What might they think of this Swedish tradition and why?

693. In Greece, Easter celebrators crack hard-boiled eggs together attempting to crack their neighbors egg first and receive good luck. Do you believe in luck? Why or why not? Would you consider yourself a lucky person and why?

694. Spain has nearly 24 straight hours of processions through the street on Easter leading up to the celebration of dancing, eating, and decorations. Do you think you could walk for 24 hours straight? Why or why not? What would be the most difficult part?

695. Vegreville, Alberta, is host to the biggest Ukrainian-style Easter egg in the world, which is over 31 feet long and weighs more than 5,000 pounds. Imagine that the egg began to roll away and you and your friends needed to catch it. Explain how you'd save the day and how you would be rewarded.

696. At the Miami MetroZoo in Florida, even animals are let in on the Easter search for goodies, with treats hidden in their cages and pens. What kind of treats do you think these animals might get? How would they get them out of the ground?

697. In Poland and Russia, a giant block of butter is shaped into a lamb sculpture to go with the Easter meal. What do you think it would be like to carve a huge mass of butter? What would you carve it into and why?

698. A San Francisco Easter parade features cows on roller blades. Describe a group of rollerblading animals going down a city street together. Where might they be going and how would people react to their journey?

699. Bermuda sends hundreds of kites into the sky on Easter weekend to act as a metaphor of Jesus Christ ascending into heaven. Describe what the sky might look like completely brightened by beautiful multi-sided kites. What kind of kite might you add to the mix?

700. Haux, France is the site of a giant Easter treat, a 4,500 egg omelet served up on Easter Monday. Imagine you had to find 1,000 people to eat this breakfast treat together. Where would you find them and how would you enjoy the egg-filled meal?

701. While Easter is a very religious holiday, many of the religious aspects are toned down for the general public, which focuses on candy and the Easter Bunny. Why do you think the religious parts of the holiday aren't emphasized in most stores and parties?

702. How would Easter change if all of the candy and Easter eggs were removed and the focus was completely on the story of the resurrection of Jesus? Do you think as many non-Christians would celebrate the occasion? Why or why not?

703. How do you think the balance between religion and the more secular aspects of Easter like candy eating will change in the next 100 years? How might new technology and a changing society affect that balance and why?

704. As society continues to become more digital, do you think fewer people will take time to paint Easter eggs and put up decorations for the holiday? Why or why not? What are some of the benefits to making things by hand instead of creating them on a screen?

705. Imagine that the world was completely painted over in Easter pastel colors. How would the colors change in the following areas: your house, school, clothes, books, and hair? How differently would these brighter colors make you feel?

706. Many people who celebrate Easter have the money and resources available to spend on decorations, candy, and gifts. Imagine that you could not afford such luxuries and that your family could only buy one Easter-specific item. What would it be and why?

707. Imagine that the Easter Bunny was a superhero who not only delivered baskets of goodies but also fought crime. How would this lawful bunny stop the bad guys? How might the holiday of Easter change to incorporate his celebrity crime-fighting status?

708. There are many songs that are sung for Christmas but hardly any for Easter. Create the titles of an album worth of made-up music for Easter. Take one of the songs and write at least a few lines of this hip-hoppy tune.

709. Imagine that major holiday figures like the Easter Bunny, Santa Claus, Cupid, the Thanksgiving Turkey, and a bunch of others have come together for a game of poker. What might these famous holiday figures talk about?

710. One of the most beautiful and expensive Easter eggs in the world has gone missing and you and your friends have been enlisted to find the thief behind the master plot. How would you come up with a list of suspects and gather clues? Would you be successful at finding the egg thief? Why or why not?

711. The word Easter may come from a pagan Anglo-Saxon goddess named Eastre, who was mentioned several times in Old English writing before the year 900 B.C.E. Imagine that you went back to the year 900 A.D. How hard might it be to understand people speaking Old English? Would they be able to understand you? Why or why not?

712. Easter was connected with the Jewish holiday of Passover from early on in its celebration and even had a similar name of Pascha around the 2nd Century A.D. What are some similarities between Easter and Passover? Why might the holidays have been so connected in the past?

713. According to the Bible, Jesus Christ died and was resurrected three days later, which is the religious foundation of the Easter holiday. Create a conversation between a Christian and a non-Christian discussing the religious and non-religious aspects of Easter.

714. As Eastre was the Anglo-Saxon goddess of the Spring, it is thought that some of the Spring aspects of Easter like bunnies, eggs, and grass may be a

carryover from old pagan traditions. How do you think the traditions of Easter might change in the next thousand years? Why?

715. The Easter Bunny originated from an Anglo-Saxon story in which Eastre changed her pet bird into a rabbit that could lay brightly colored eggs to entertain children. How do you think rabbits would be treated differently if they could all lay colorful eggs? Why?

716. The mythical bunny later became associated with Easter in writings in Germany in the 1500s, and by the 1800s, the Easter Bunny's likeness appeared in sugary pastry form. What are some different kinds of desserts you could picture in the form of an Easter Bunny? Would any of them be as good as a chocolate bunny? Why or why not?

717. While Easter was celebrated as a religious holiday for many years in the United States, the secular aspects like the Easter Bunny and candy baskets were not widely celebrated in the U.S. until after the Civil War. How do you think Easter would be different if it wasn't celebrated in the United States?

718. Wearing new and beautiful clothes for Easter started as a Spring tradition in ancient Iran, China, and Germanic countries. It was eventually made into an Easter decree around the year 325 C.E. by the Roman emperor Constantine. Imagine that you only wore new clothes once a year, on Easter. Why might that set of clothes be special to you?

719. During the earliest Easter celebrations, things like new clothes, candy, and parades would likely have been frowned upon. Why do you think these entertaining aspects of the modern holiday would not have been as accepted?

720. The largest candy Easter egg ever made was nearly 9,000 pounds of chocolate and marshmallow. Describe how you and a large amount of friends might go about trying to eat such a deliciously huge treat.

EARTH DAY

721. Do you think it's important to have a holiday to concentrate on the environment and the health of planet Earth? Why or why not?

722. What are some of the ways that you can help to take care of the environment more effectively? How hard would it be for you to put those changes into practice? Why?

723. If we are unable to improve how we treat the planet, how do you think the earth will look in a thousand years? How different would life be for a person your age to live in such a polluted environment?

724. Create a made-up story using the following words: planet, trash, cleaning, and green.

725. What would be some good ways for you and your family to celebrate Earth Day? Do you think that everybody in your family would be on board? If so, what would each family member do to be involved? If not, who do you think would drag his or her feet and why?

726. One of the coolest environmental habits is the practice of recycling. What are some ways that you could recycle bottles, cans, and other materials that can end up landfills?

727. Imagine that you and your friends were in a room with one of the biggest polluters in the world. What would you say to this person to make him or her change his or her ways? Would you be successful? Why or why not?

728. Have you ever planted a tree, flower or other kind of plant? If so, what was it and did you enjoy getting your hands dirty and why? If not, what would be your plant of choice to put into the ground to watch grow? Why?

729. Hundreds of years ago, people didn't know as much about the environment and sent coal dust and other pollutants out into the environment. How do you think the world would be different today if we protected the environment from the beginning?

730. Imagine that you lived in a perfectly green world. Describe how the air, water, and ground feel in a place without any kind of pollution.

731. As pollution continues to increase from year to year, how do you think the planet Earth will look for your children and your children's children? How can you personally contribute to making the earth a cleaner place in the future?

732. While progress is important for better toys, games, and activities, it tends to add more pollution. Is it better to have more entertaining, advanced and convenient objects and activities or is it better to have a cleaner planet and why?

733. Imagine that you and a team of community service workers are picking up trash by the side of the road. What kind of trash do you see? How does it make you feel to see and pick up the rubbish that other people could have thrown away?

734. One way to treat the Earth better is to reduce how much electricity we use. What are all of the things you do at home that use electricity? How would you occupy yourself on an electricity-free night?

735. Imagine that you and a group of friends have discovered a new animal species in the rainforest. The only issue is that it's a section of forest that is about to be cut down by a local company. What do you do and why?

736. Before environmental regulations were in place, companies dumped their waste and chemicals into the nearby water or in the ground. Why do you think they were so irresponsible with their waste management? How would you have done it differently?

737. Write out a plan for a nature vacation that is absent of electricity and technology. Where would you go, what would you do, and how would you enjoy it?

738. Create a conversation between two extremely tall trees as they watch pollution float by. What are their opinions on the passing chemical gases? What do they remember about a cleaner and healthier time?

739. Do you think recycling is an important way to help the planet? Why or why not? What are some of the things you and your family recycle?

740. Imagine if everyone in your town rode bikes instead of driving cars. How would it change the town? Would it decrease the amount of pollution in the area? Why or why not?

741. Spending time with nature is a common Earth Day activity. Where would you go to celebrate nature near your town? What would you do there and why?

742. One way to spend Earth Day is to join a group in picking up trash from a beach or a street. Who would you recruit to join you in this activity and how would you make it fun?

743. Many organizations hold fundraisers for Earth-related causes on the holiday, such as concerts, fun runs, and bake sales. What kind of fundraiser would you want to hold? What organization would you donate the proceeds to and why?

744. Imagine that you have been asked to create a new environmental movie for Earth Day. What would the movie be about and how would you go about filming it with an unlimited budget and access to the best and brightest celebrities?

745. The organization Project Aware holds underwater diving events to pick up waste in the water during Earth Day. Do you think trash in the ocean would be a problem? Why or why not?

746. Imagine that your entire classroom has become a forum of discussion about the Earth for the entire day. What topics might you and your peers discuss? Would some people be resistant to changing their anti-Earth habits and if so, why?

747. Learning about the Earth is just as important as teaching other people what you've learned. Who is someone you could teach something about the Earth that you learned today? How might this person react to your new knowledge?

748. Planting new trees to make up for the ones that have been torn down is an important activity on Earth Day. Create a conversation between an old tree and a young tree talking about the holiday. What might they discuss and why?

749. While some people take an hour off of electricity during Earth Day, there are still people in the world who rarely use electricity. How would your life be

different if you didn't have electricity? What would you do with your free time and why?

750. What do you think is the most important way to celebrate Earth Day? Why don't more people take the opportunity to honor the planet like that for the holiday?

751. What aspects of the Earth are most important to you and why? Which of those could be threatened if we don't take good enough care of our planet? Why?

752. Imagine that you have come up with an anti-pollution device that would immediately solve a good portion of the world's issues with air pollution. How would the invention work, how would the world put it to good use, and what would be the result?

753. Short of coming up with a miraculous invention, what are some of the things the world needs to do to make sure it stays green as opposed to dark with pollution? What are the obstacles that might hold people back from lending a hand? Why?

754. You have been asked to put together an anti-trash squad in your town. What materials would you need, which people would you recruit, and how would you most effectively get things done? How successful would your squad be at cleaning up the streets? Why?

755. Imagine that the world was so polluted you actually needed to wear a mask whenever you left your house. What activities might you not be able to do in such a dirty existence? How might it affect your friendships, sports teams and your family?

756. Why are plants such an important part of the earth's ecosystem? What are some ways in which you can help the plant-life in your town? How might your efforts end up making a difference?

757. You have developed a new, unlimited energy source that can be used in place of coal, oil, and natural gas. The fuel is safe for the environment and could change the planet drastically. In what ways would your new energy source help the world? Why might some people be resistant to using this helpful innovation?

758. You and a group of friends have set a goal to plant one million trees over the next 25 years. How would you go about enacting this ambitious plan? What might result from all of your hard efforts?

759. Imagine that you had to give a speech to a group of company presidents to convince them to improve their companies' environmental practices. What might you say to them, how might they react, and what would be the end result?

760. Earth has been completely used up and the human population needs to escape to find another world. What would it be like to pack everything up into a spaceship and search for a new planet with the capability for water, plants, and humans? What would be the most difficult parts and why?

761. Campaigns to save the earth and the environment were practically non-existent before the 1960s. Why do you think it took until then for people to protest pollution and to champion environmental causes?

762. The publication of Rachel Carson's *Silent Spring* warned the public about the dangers of chemicals in the environment. Have you ever warned somebody about something that was dangerous? Did that person listen to you? Why or why not?

763. Carson advocated for more natural as opposed to chemical ways to take care of problems like plant-harming insects. Imagine you decided to go chemical-free for an entire week. What are some things you'd have to give up? How would you successfully last the whole week?

764. Shortly after Carson's book was released, many environmental groups were formed in the government and in the non-profit sector. Create a conversation between two concerned parents who are considering a fundraising party for one of these groups.

765. A Wisconsin senator named Gaylord Perry was inspired by a 1969 oil spill to create what would become the first Earth Day in 1970. Imagine if an oil spill occurred in your town. How would the wildlife be affected? What would you do about it? Why?

766. The 20 million people who supported the first Earth Day led to the creation of new laws like the Clean Air Act. If you could rally a large amount of people to create a new law, what would it be and why?

767. Twenty years later, one of the original Earth Day coordinators, Denis Hayes, helped to build a worldwide celebration for the holiday. How do you think Hayes was able to recruit the entire world for the causes of recycling and the environment? Why might it be tough to get everyone on the same page?

768. Write a poem about your thoughts on nature and why a holiday geared toward the environment might be important.

769. Of all the environmental issues over the years, including chemical pesticides, oil spills, recycling, clean energy, etc., which do you think is the most important and why?

770. In 2012, Earth Day organizers launched an effort to plant one million trees throughout the world. How do you think planting that many trees would change the environment? Why?

ARBOR DAY

771. J. Sterling Morton, a nature lover and journalist, started spreading his enthusiasm for trees when he became the editor of a Nebraska newspaper in the 1850s. What subjects might you talk about if you were in control of a type of

news? Would you use your influence for improving the world or helping yourself? Why?

772. After becoming a member of the Nebraska government, Morton continued to stress the need for trees and eventually put together the tree-planting holiday Arbor Day on April 10, 1872. Imagine that you had an idea so good that you'd be willing to spend decades on achieving it. What might such an idea be? How would you make it a reality?

773. Over one million trees were planted on that first unofficial Arbor Day. How long do you think it would take you, your family, and your friends to plant that many trees? What would be the most difficult part of this agricultural work and why?

774. The holiday spread throughout many other states and is now celebrated in all 50 states and in many countries. Imagine that you started a trend that spread to every other person in your school or neighborhood. What might that trend be? How would you feel being the person who started such a popular way of doing things?

775. One reason the holiday became so popular is because of the many benefits of trees. What are some positive aspects of trees that you can think of? Why might having millions of new trees throughout the world each year be important?

776. While trees are important to humans, they also serve as the home to many different types of organisms in nature. Imagine that you were a small creature living in a tree. What might your day-to-day life be like? How would you show your appreciation for the tree you lived in?

777. Even though trees are so important, many of them are cut down every year throughout the world for various reasons. What are some of the reasons trees get chopped down? What could happen in a wooded area if trees don't get replanted?

778. You have been asked to hold an Arbor Day festival in your town. What events might you organize to celebrate the holiday? How would you get everybody in the area to attend? What would have to happen at the event for you to consider it a success and why?

779. Arbor Day isn't just about planting trees, because the trees that are already planted may need help too. Imagine that you were a tree doctor who went around tending to sick trees. How might you make a sick tree become healthy again? Why?

780. There is a tree in Inyo County, California, named Methuselah that is thought to be over 4,800 years old. Imagine that you were Methuselah and you were able to watch the world change dramatically over nearly 5,000 years of life. What would be some major events that stuck out to you? How would you feel about living for so long and why?

Bryan Cohen

CINCO DE MAYO, MOTHER'S DAY AND MEMORIAL DAY

CINCO DE MAYO

781. Cinco de Mayo is a holiday that commemorates a Mexican battle in which the country defeated a French army nearly twice its size. Describe an example from your life when you knew someone who prevailed despite difficult odds. Why do you think most people love an underdog story?

782. While Cinco de Mayo is popular in the United States, it isn't heavily celebrated in Mexico. What might have held the holiday back from becoming popular in Mexico? Why do you think the holiday took off in the U.S.?

783. Cinco de Mayo has become a major holiday for the celebration of Mexican heritage in the U.S. What are your favorite aspects of Mexican culture and why?

784. The holiday became more popular when major companies learned how they could make money from it. Imagine that you and your friends have found a way to earn some cash from promoting an obscure holiday. What would the holiday be and how would you earn your fortune?

785. Mexican food, a major part any Cinco de Mayo celebration, has become much more popular in the United States over the last few decades. What is your favorite type of ethnic food and why do you enjoy it so much?

786. Denver's Cinco de Mayo celebration is full of Mexican music and dancing including mariachi songs, Tejano-style pop, and sultry salsa dancers. Do you think dancing is a big part of the American culture? Why or why not?

787. In Nevada, part of the Cinco de Mayo celebration includes art, entertainment and Mexican-style wrestling called lucha libre. Imagine that you filled for a masked Mexican wrestler as part of the festival. Describe the experience from beginning to end.

788. While many people assume that Cinco de Mayo is the same as Mexican Independence Day, that holiday actually occurs in September. Why do you think the May holiday has become a bigger deal in the U.S. even though it only celebrates a single military victory?

789. In Chandler, Arizona, the Chihuahua is a Cinco de Mayo festival in which the tiny hairless pups engage in adorable races. What might it look like to see Chihuahuas racing down the street? Would you enjoy such an event? Why or why not?

790. While Hispanic culture has become more accepted in the United States, there is still rampant discrimination against Latin Americans. How do you think

Cinco de Mayo could be used to reduce that discrimination? What might have to happen for such racism to be thrown out the window and why?

MOTHER'S DAY

791. What do you think is the most special gift you could ever give your mother for Mother's Day? How do you think she would react when you gave it to her?

792. What are some of the qualities that make up an awesome mom? Why do you think those qualities are so important to being the best mother possible?

793. You and your friends have come together to create a scrumptious Mother's Day brunch for all of your moms. What foods do you serve at this mom festival? Is the meal as good as your mother's cooking? Why or why not?

794. Would you describe being a mom as a hard job or an easy job? Would you ever want to take on your mom's responsibilities for a week or two? Why or why not?

795. While it's nice to have a holiday for our moms, there are things we can do every day to make our moms' lives easier. What are a few things you can do to help to make your mom happier?

796. Create a made-up story using the following words: breakfast, hug, dishes, and motherly.

797. What does your mom do for a living? Have you ever been to where your mom works? What were some of the reactions from your mom's co-workers when you visited?

798. One of the things moms do best is give nicknames. What are some of the nicknames your mom has given you over the years? How and why do you think she came up with them?

799. Imagine that your mom and all the other moms on your block were actually aliens pretending to be humans! What planet would your mom be from and would she have any secret alien powers?

800. Who are some of your mom's best friends in the world? What kinds of activities do they do together? Why do you think your mom gets along with her friends so well?

801. Imagine what kind of gifts your mom gave her mother when she was your age on this special day. How would your mom enjoy getting the same kind of gifts from you?

802. What are some words that would best describe your mom? Do you think she would agree with the words you've chosen? Why or why not?

803. Which of the following gifts would your mom enjoy the most: chocolate, flowers, jewelry, a purse, or a vacation? Why would she enjoy that gift in particular?

804. Imagine that you've found out that your mom is an actual superhero who goes around fighting crime. What would her super powers be? How would you look at her differently and why?

805. Create a dialogue between you and your mom talking about Mother's Day. What would the two of you talk about and why?

806. Mothers love to give advice. What is the best advice your mom has given you and why?

807. What do you think it was like for your mom to carry you around in her belly for nine months? What was fun about having you growing inside of her and what might have been tough?

808. Describe the perfect Mother's Day celebration for your mom from the moment she wakes up to the second she goes to bed. What are some ways you could bring that perfect celebration to reality?

809. If you wrote a book about your mom, what creative title would you give it and why? What are some of the stories you might tell about your mom within its pages?

810. What are some of your mom's favorite hobbies and why does she like them so much? How might you participate in those activities?

811. One of the top choices for celebrating Mother's Day is taking your mom out to brunch. What kind of restaurant would your mother enjoy the most for the special day? What food would she get and why do you think she likes it so much?

812. Some kids and husbands treat mothers to a relaxing day of spa treatments and massages. Imagine that you and your family have tried to turn your house into a spa to save some money. What would your mother think and why?

813. Other mothers use the holiday as an excuse to go wine-tasting in the countryside. Is your mother more of a country, suburban, or city person? Why?

814. Concerts and other artistic performances are a must for the mother interested in culture. What kinds of music does your mom like? How does her taste differ from your own? Why do you think she likes the music she likes?

815. If your mother could take a trip with her friends anywhere in the world on Mother's Day, where would it be and why? Would the location be different if she was bringing you and the rest of the family with her? Why?

816. Some active mothers take the opportunity to race on Mother's Day with their loved ones in a 5K or triathlon. Would your mother be interested in such an event? Why or why not?

817. There are many wonderful gifts that you could get your mother for the holiday, but everyone can make mistakes. What are some of the worst ideas you can think of to give your mother on Mother's Day? Why would they be so bad?

818. You and your family members have forgotten to get flowers for your mother and the only florist in town says that he's sold out. What do you do to make sure your mom has a bouquet of roses waiting for her when she wakes up?

819. In some countries in the past, Mother's Day was celebrated to encourage families to have more kids. How would your family be different if you had double or triple the amount of brothers and sisters? How difficult would such a family be on your mother?

820. In Yugoslavia, Mother's Day seems more for the children then the moms themselves. The children have a tradition of tying up their mother and ransoming her freedom for gifts. What would your mom do if you tied her up? Why might it not be such a good idea?

821. What are some of the things a person has to learn before becoming a good mother? Do you think most people learn those skills beforehand or do they figure it out as they go along? Why?

822. What kind of advice do you think your mom would give you about being a parent? What would she say are the toughest aspects and what would she say are the most rewarding parts? Do you think you'd take her advice later in life? Why or why not?

823. While moms and dads may both have to do a lot of work when taking care of a child, it's only the mother who can have a baby growing inside of her. What do you think might be the toughest parts of pregnancy and why would they be so difficult?

824. Imagine that you came home from school to find out that your mom was pregnant! How would this news change your family? How would you help your mom over the next nine months?

825. Name some of your mom's favorites in the following areas: hobbies, books, television shows, movies, and songs. Have you ever tried out some of your mother's favorites? Did you enjoy them yourself? Why or why not?

826. Imagine that for mother's day you decided to get your mom all of her favorite things. How would you get all of the gifts together? Would you need any help and from who? What would her reaction be to your massive multi-part gift and why?

827. What are some occurrences that make your mom laugh? Why do you think they make her so happy? How would you describe her laugh? What are some things you can do on Mother's Day to make her laugh like that?

828. Think about a time in which your mom took care of you. Why did you need her help and what did she do to make you feel better? How might you express your appreciation for what she did? What would her reaction be?

829. What are some ways in which your mother is unique from all other mothers? What are some ways in which she is similar to other moms you know?

830. What are some of the traits, habits and personality quirks that you've had passed down to you from your mother? What other aspects of her would you like to inherit from her as you grow up and why?

831. In the 17th Century, the British celebrated a holiday called Mothering Day that allowed mothers in all social classes to return home and visit their families. What do you think it would be like for a mother not to be able to be with her family most of the year? Why might she have to do so in the first place?

832. The first American idea of Mother's Day came in 1870 when Julia Ward Howe called for an international day of motherhood and peace. How might it have been hard to be a mother only a few years after the Civil War? Why do you think Howe connected moms and peace?

833. Howe's attempt at Mother's Day lasted just over a decade and never became the holiday she hoped it would. Imagine that you tried to start a movement and that it didn't quite work out. How would it make you feel and why?

834. In 1908, Anna Reeves Jarvis campaigned for a new Mother's Day which actually caught on. She wanted all mothers to be celebrated for their hard work, including mothers who had passed away. Do you think it's important for all mothers to be honored? Why or why not?

835. Despite Jarvis's success at creating Mother's Day, she wasn't happy with how commercialized it became with Hallmark cards and gifts. Do you think that what she created was positive for mothers even though she didn't like how it turned out? Why?

836. Restaurants are at their busiest on Mother's Day because so many children take their mothers out on the holiday. Where would you take your mom out to eat on Mother's Day? Why would you choose that place in particular?

837. Long-distance phone calls are also at their peak during the motherly holiday. How do you think the holiday would be different if you were away from home on Mother's Day? Why?

838. Over 70 countries celebrate Mother's Day around the world. How do you think the celebration might differ from place to place? Do you think your mother would enjoy the U.S. celebration or another country's celebration better? Why?

839. Even though the American Mother's Day is a unique creation, some connect the holiday to the celebration of ancient Middle Eastern goddesses over

6,000 year ago. How do you think a celebration of mothers would be different all those years ago?

840. How do you think Mother's Day will change in the next 6,000 years? Do you think mothers will still be honored? Why or why not?

MEMORIAL DAY

841. Why do you think there are multiple holidays that honor the military? How might you show respect to the Armed Forces in a different way than you did on the other holidays?

842. One major responsibility of the military is to protect the country. Who are some of the people outside of the military who protect you and why do they do it? Are there any people you protect? How do you protect them?

843. Members of the military risk their lives to preserve the lives of citizens of the United States and other countries. What does being a citizen mean to you? How do you think being a U.S. citizen differs from being a citizen of another country?

844. Protecting lives is a major responsibility. What are some responsibilities that you've had in your life? What kind of responsibilities might you have when you get older?

845. Imagine that you had to go through intense training for a career or a competition. What kind of things would you do to train? How would you keep yourself going when you got tired?

846. Describe what you think the inside of a submarine might look like. Make sure to include a description of all the officers trying to move around inside.

847. When you get older, you'll be allowed to vote for or against certain laws and politicians. Why might it be important to be able to vote as opposed to having a king or dictator come up with the laws for us?

848. Imagine how hard it would be if you had a family member in the Armed Forces for months or years at a time. How would you keep in touch with this person? How would you feel about him or her being away?

849. Memorial Day weekend often kicks off with a big summer blockbuster movie at the local theater. Do you and your family go to the movies on Memorial Day weekend, or do you have other activities planned? What would you do to celebrate if you had a choice and why?

850. One of the most important symbols of the country and its military is the American flag. What does the flag mean to you? How do you feel when you see it? Why?

851. Memorial Day is in some ways a very solemn holiday to remember the service of soldiers who are no longer with us. Why do you

think many people think of it more as a time for parties, movies, and vacations?

852. One of the original traditions of Memorial Day was the decoration of the gravestones of soldiers. How might you decorate the memorial of a fallen soldier? What would the soldier's family think of your decorating?

853. Why do you think it's important to remember people who did a great service for the United States even long after they're gone? What are some good ways to honor their memory?

854. Create a conversation between two people in their twenties deciding whether or not they should join the military. What might be some of their reasons for and what might be some of their reasons against?

855. Joining the military takes a lot of hard work and training. What is the hardest thing you've ever had to work for? Why was it difficult and how did you train to get better at it?

856. Imagine that you and a relative who served in the military are looking through some old pictures related to his or her time in the service. What might you two talk about and why?

857. What do you think it means to be patriotic? Would you say that you are patriotic, yourself? Why or why not?

858. We often think about frontline soldiers when we think about the military, but there are plenty of behind the scenes, like nurses and code breakers, who also put themselves in danger. What do you think it would be like to support the troops directly in those positions? Would you still be scared? Why or why not?

859. How might you explain Memorial Day to a person from a foreign country? What parts about the holiday might be difficult to understand?

860. You have been chosen to create a very red, white, and blue meal for Memorial Day. What kinds of food do you serve? How will your guests enjoy your patriotic delicacies?

861. Many museums and parks offer special exhibits on Memorial Day to give attention to the U.S. military service. Do you think it's important to remember the contribution of the military long after they're gone? Why or why not?

862. Each Memorial Day at the Arlington National Cemetery, American flags are placed at every service member's grave stone and guarded to ensure the graves are not disturbed. What do you think is the meaning of this tradition? Why might it be a touching ceremony for some?

863. The National Memorial Day Parade in Washington, D.C., includes entertainment but is more well known for its tributes to various wars and branches of the military. Do you think it's necessary to have a balance of fun and seriousness on a holiday like Memorial Day? Why or why not?

864. Ports around the country celebrate boating and sailing festivals on Memorial Day. Imagine that you could own any boat you wanted. What kind would it be, what would you do with it, and why?

865. The Indianapolis 500 is a racing event over Memorial Day weekend that is attended by approximately 400,000 people. Imagine sitting inside one of those cars zipping around the track. What might it feel like to go so fast? Would you enjoy it? Why or why not?

866. Mount Vernon, Virginia, boasts a Sunset Celebration on Memorial Day weekend to witness the setting sun on George Washington's home. Imagine sitting down with the first President and chatting about the holiday. What might you discuss and why?

867. There are monuments all around the country that serve as fitting places to honor fallen soldiers on Memorial Day. Imagine that you were in charge of creating your own memorial. What would it look like, who would it honor and why?

868. America's national parks are frequently visited on Memorial Day, giving visitors the chance to see the most beautiful parts of the country. How do you think seeing such a breathtaking part of the U.S. would make you feel and why?

869. The barbecue is a Memorial Day tradition, but it's not always directly connected to the honoring of America's troops. What are three ways that a standard barbecue could be more connected with the roots of the holiday? Do you think the changes would be for the better or the worse and why?

870. While there are many Memorial Day traditions, one of the most frequent modern practices is to go on a vacation. What is a vacation you and your family could go on that would be equally patriotic and enjoyable? Why might such a trip be more fulfilling than one purely for fun?

871. Memorial Day is a holiday meant to commemorate the lives of service members who have passed away. Do you think it's important to honor the deceased? Why or why not?

872. There are multiple war memorials around the country to honor the fallen soldiers of World War I, World War II, Vietnam, and more. People will go to these memorials to pray, lay flowers, or just look at the names of their family members. Why do people act in these ways around memorials? How do you think you would spend your time at a war memorial? Why?

873. You have stumbled upon the diary of a soldier from the Civil War, over a century ago. What are some of the entries about? What might you learn from

such an intimate portrayal of a deadly war? How might you try to honor this long-gone soldier's memory? Why?

874. Most countries have a similar holiday to Memorial Day in which they honor their fallen service members. How do you think the occasion might differ in other nations and why? What might it be like to visit a war memorial when touring a foreign country?

875. There are many service members who died during major wars who were not in the act of fighting. These people include doctors, nurses, lawyers and clergymen. How do you think these people should be honored on Memorial Day? Why might they have been willing to put themselves at risk for jobs they could have outside of the military?

876. While some people lost members of their family in the military decades in the past, there are also those who lost them in the past month or year. How would you comfort someone who recently lost a loved one? Why?

877. Imagine that everyone fighting for the U.S. military gave up and went home. What might some of the consequences be of having no military whatsoever? How does this demonstrate the importance of having active service members who are willing to keep America free?

878. Imagine that you have been asked to speak at a wreath-laying taking place at a nearby war memorial. What points might you want to hit during your speech? What would be the most important objective of your talk and why?

879. Even if you have no family members or friends who have been anywhere close to the military, it's still possible to honor those who have served. What are some ways you can participate in honoring fallen troops on Memorial Day? What might your efforts mean to someone who has lost a member of his or her family? Why?

880. You have several million dollars that you've raised to start a foundation to support members of the military. In what way would your foundation help the military? How would you personally participate in the organization? How would people feel about what the group does and why?

881. On Memorial Day, many people visit cemeteries to honor those who died in all wars. Have you ever visited a cemetery? How did it make you feel and why?

882. Memorial Day was first called Decoration Day because people decorated gravestones with flags and flowers. What do you think is the meaning of such decorations? Do you think the graveyard decorations are important? Why or why not?

883. In the early days of these decoration days, participants often brought a different meal as part of a potluck dinner. Have you ever been to a potluck dinner? What foods would be present at your ideal potluck and why?

884. Memorial Day originated after the Civil War and many freed African-American slaves participated in a major decoration and cleaning ceremony to honor the deceased Union soldiers. Why do you think it was so important for the newly free men to honor the soldiers?

885. While Memorial Day originally was meant to honor soldiers from the Civil War, it eventually took on meaning to honor all fallen veterans. Do you think it's important to remember those who fought in the Civil War in particular? Why or why not?

886. Create a conversation between two wreaths of flowers placed on adjacent gravestones in a military cemetery. What might these important decorations have to say to each other and why?

887. Memorial Day was placed toward the end of May partly to ensure that flowers would be in full bloom. What are some other things that occur at the end of May? Which end-of-May activities do you look forward to the most?

888. One of the resolutions of Memorial Day is that the living continue to fight for liberty and justice. What do you think it means to fight for liberty and justice for all? How might you support liberty and justice in your everyday life?

889. Nora Fontaine Davidson, a schoolteacher, is thought to be one of the inspirations for Memorial Day. Imagine that your actions somehow inspired a holiday. What kind of holiday might it be? Would your family be proud of your inspirational ways? Why or why not?

890. Davidson was known for founding a school and a hospital, and for decorating the graves of soldiers. What are some things you want to be remembered for? How would you like to be described by your past teachers and your friends and family? Why?

FATHER'S DAY, INDEPENDENCE DAY AND RAMADAN

FATHER'S DAY

891. One of the most traditional Father's Day gifts to give to a dad is a tie. If you added up all of the ties people got for their dads during the holiday, you'd end up with millions of ties! What would you do with a giant mountain of ties and why would you do it?

892. Some dads have the image of being rugged and outdoorsy. Would you say that your dad is like that? If so, how did he get that way? If not, how would you describe your dad?

893. Imagine that you went back in time to hang out with your dad at your age. How do you think he'd be different from the way he is today? Do you think the two of you would get along?

894. What does your family do to celebrate Father's Day? Describe your festivities from the beginning to the end of the day. Do you think he enjoys all the attention? Why or why not?

895. Write a made-up story using the following words: lawnmower, tools, manly, and smile.

896. Does your dad do chores around the house? If so, what chore do you think he's best at? If not, which of your chores do you wish he would do and why?

897. What are some of the ways in which your dad is the same as his dad? What are some of the ways in which he's different? How do you think you'll be different from your dad when you grow up?

898. If you could have any famous celebrity as your dad, who would he be and why? How do you think Father's Day would be different with such a well-known person as your pop?

899. Describe one of the following in great detail: Your dad's tool collection, your dad's wardrobe, your dad's computer station, or your dad's favorite foods.

900. Imagine that you are planning a surprise Father's Day party for your dad. Who would you invite and why? What foods would you serve, what music would you play, and what activities would you set up? Do you think your dad would be surprised? Why or why not?

901. What are some of the activities you like to do with your dad? Why do you enjoy them so much?

902. What are some of the lessons your father has taught you that you'd want to teach to your son or daughter? Why do you think those lessons are important?

903. How is your dad unique compared to some of the other dads you know? How is your dad similar to these other fathers?

904. One responsibility of a dad is to protect his children. How does your dad protect you and your family? How often do you need protection?

905. Seeing your child for the first time can be quite a powerful experience. What do you think your dad's reaction was when he first saw you as a baby? Why do you imagine he reacted that way?

906. Imagine that you've decided to improve your behavior for an entire week as your Father's Day present. What would you do differently to be more well-behaved? Why don't you act that way all of the time?

907. Who do you think are the most famous fathers in history? How did they become so famous? How does your father compare to them?

908. Create a conversation between two ties in a clothing store on the day before Father's Day. Do you think they want to be purchased for a dad, or would they rather stay with the other ties? Why?

909. You have been given the responsibility of cooking your father's favorite meal. What are some of the ingredients that you will need? How successful are you at feeding your dad the food he enjoys the most?

910. Write a poem to your dad thanking him for all that he's done for you. Why do you think he'll appreciate the poem?

911. While brunch is key on Mother's Day, many fathers would rather be grilling. What would the ideal barbecue be like for your dad? What would he cook, who would be there and how would you help?

912. Would your dad rather go on a relaxing fishing trip or visit a loud sporting event like a monster truck rally? Why would he make that decision and how would his choice fit his personality?

913. In Australia, some fathers are given Father of the Year Awards. What award do you think your dad could be in the running for and why?

914. Father's Day in Germany can involve male hiking trips carrying food and drink through the trails or mountains. What would such a trip be like with your dad and his friends? What kind of foods might be found in your wagon?

915. Some dads like to go see old stuff on Father's Day, like a black-and-white movie, a museum, or some antique cars. What are some of the old things your dad might enjoy looking at? Do you think he likes things from the past more than things in the present? Why?

916. Would your dad rather spend time with you and your family on Father's Day or would he rather have time alone? Why?

917. Imagine that you have created a scavenger hunt for your dad to find his way to a major Father's Day party. What kind of clues might you leave for him

that only he would know? Would he get there on time for the party? Why or why not?

918. Describe the perfect Father's Day gift for your dad. How would you get your hands on such an item and what would he think of it?

919. Ultimately, Father's Day is about spending time with your father. What is the most amount of time you've spent with your dad consecutively? Did you learn anything new from spending so much time with him? Why or why not?

920. Father's Day doesn't just have to be for your dad, but the holiday can celebrate all the dads you know. Who are some other dads can think of that deserve praise for the holiday? How are they important to you?

921. What are some of the things a person has to learn before becoming a good father? Do you think most people learn those skills beforehand or do they figure it out as they go along? Why?

922. Who would you say is the world's most famous dad? How did this father become so well known? In what ways do you think this special dad celebrates the Father's Day holiday and why?

923. There's an old saying that goes, "father knows best." Where do you think the saying came from? Would you agree with that phrase? Do you think that your dad usually does know best? Why or why not?

924. What are some areas in which you'd say your dad is an expert? How did he come to learn this knowledge? What are some subjects that your dad knows nothing about? Have you ever taught your dad something? Why or why not?

925. What are some of your dad's favorites in the following areas: hobbies, books, television shows, movies, and songs. Have you ever tried out some of your dad's favorites? Did you enjoy them yourself? Why or why not?

926. How do your favorite things to do differ from your dad's? Would you say that you've been influenced to like or dislike something from him? Why or why not?

927. What are some accomplishments you've had that have made your dad the most proud? How does he usually react when he's proud of you? What are some things that you can do on Father's Day to make your dad proud of you?

928. Think about a time in which your dad bought or gave you something. What was it you needed and how did you ask him for it? How could you show your appreciation for what he gave you? What would his reaction be?

929. How would you rate your dad's skill levels at the following activities: singing, dancing, acting, joking, and weightlifting? Which do you think he's the best at and why? When you're an adult, do you think you'll be better or worse at these areas then him? Why?

930. What are some of the traits, habits and personality quirks that you've had passed down to you from your father? What other aspects of him would you like to inherit from him as you grow up and why?

931. The first recorded Father's Day honored over 300 men who passed away in a coal mine in West Virginia in 1908 and the state has claimed credit for the first celebration of the holiday. Have you ever taken credit for being the first to come up with an idea? Why do you think it's important to say that you started an idea or movement?

932. Sonora Louise Smart Dodd started campaigning in 1909 for the Father's Day we know today to honor fathers, especially her father, who raised Dodd and her five siblings alone. Do you think it would be hard to raise six children as a single parent? Why or why not?

933. Another reason Dodd promoted the holiday, which first took place in 1910, was because of the gaining popularity of Mother's Day. Imagine if there was a Mother's Day without a Father's Day. Do you think fathers would feel left out? Why or why not?

934. While the holiday faded after Dodd took time to go to college, it eventually picked back up in the 1930s when she gained the support of tie manufacturers and other male goods manufacturers. Why would a tie company have a stake in Father's Day?

935. Create a conversation between two male gift company presidents who are considering spending advertising money on Father's Day in its early stages. What are their opinions about fathers and why might they make a major push for the holiday?

936. After multiple governmental attempts to make Father's Day official, President Richard Nixon made it a national holiday in 1972. Imagine you and your friends could come up with a holiday to propose to the President. What holiday would you think up and do you think it would pass? Why or why not?

937. If you were a father, what kind of gifts might you want to celebrate the special day? Which would be more important: gifts or having a chance to spend time with your family and why?

938. A growing phenomenon is the stay-at-home dad, a father who tends to the house and children while the mother is out working. Why do you think this used to be more rare? Do you think caring for the family is less or more important than working at a job? Why?

939. Do you think that your father enjoys the Father's Day holiday? Why? What might he like and dislike about the special day?

940. Father's Day is celebrated throughout the world on many different days and in many different ways. If you could invent a new tradition for Father's Day, what would it be and why would you create it? How would your father feel about the new tradition?

INDEPENDENCE DAY

941. Create a made-up 4th of July story using the following words: fireworks, summer, hamburgers, and independence.

942. What do you think our founding fathers like George Washington would think about the modern-day Independence Day? What would they like about it and what would they dislike?

943. Why do you think Independence Day is important? Do you and your family do anything special to celebrate the holiday? Why or why not?

944. Imagine a 4th of July barbecue with all of your friends and family. Who would be there, what would you eat, and what would you do for fun?

945. You are an American flag flying proudly above the town at the top of a flag pole. How do you feel on Independence Day and do you do anything special during the holiday?

946. You have been picked to march in a national 4th of July parade! Why were you picked for this special honor? What is it like to be the center of such patriotic attention?

947. Describe the best fireworks display you've ever seen. What were the sights, sounds, and smells surrounding the colorful event?

948. Who do you think deserves the most credit on the 4th of July for helping to make the country an independent nation? How do you honor these important people?

949. What do you think is the most essential 4th of July food and why is it so important? How would the holiday change without that special food item?

950. Different countries around the world have been independent much longer than the United States. How do you think the country will change in the next hundred or thousand years?

951. What are some of the things that freedom means to you? How would your life change if you and your family members no longer had freedom?

952. Imagine that you have been entered into a patriotic costume contest. What kind of clothing would you wear to look as patriotic as possible? Describe your outfit from top to bottom.

953. Describe the different types of fireworks you've seen. Why do some fireworks explode right away while others make crazy sounds and shoot way up into the air before detonating?

954. You hear a sound at your window and are surprised to find a Bald Eagle, one of the symbols of the United States, at your window to deliver a message. What is the message? How do you go about delivering that message to everyone you know?

955. Write a dialogue between two fireworks before they're about to be fired off into the sky. How well do these explosive personalities get along and why?

956. Have you ever visited your state capital or the capital of the entire country? What sights might you want to see when you visit and why would you want to visit them?

957. Why is the American flag sometimes called the "stars and stripes?" What other nicknames might you give to one of the major symbols of the United States?

958. Imagine that you are a master chef getting ready to cook for a 4th of July celebration. What kind of foods will you cook and why? Do you have any special way of preparing them to set them apart?

959. Imagine that you were at the signing of the Declaration of Independence way back in 1776. Describe the other people there, including the most famous founding fathers in our history. Would you be surprised by anything you see there? Why or why not?

960. How would a celebration for Independence Day have been different 100 years ago? How would a 4th of July celebration be different 100 years in the future?

961. The Declaration of Independence can be heard from the balcony of the Old State House in Boston during the holiday. What do you think it was like to hear the declaration read for the first time back in 1776? How might it have affected you?

962. Imagine that your family celebrated Independence Day like the Nathan's Hot Dog Eating Contest, by having an eating challenge! What food items would your family compete with, who is likely to win, and why?

963. In Newport Harbor, California, boat lovers unite to race patriotically decorated tugboats, classics, and more in a watery July 4th competition. What kind of boat would you use to race? What kind of training might you have to do to win?

964. Remembering the old-fashioned United States is easier in Old Sturbridge Village, Massachusetts, with the Stepping Back in Time Event. People dress in vintage costumes and take part in old-timey activities. What would you enjoy the most about such an event and why?

965. There's nothing quite like seeing a parade of red, white, and blue floats and flags making their way down a city street. What modern touches might you add to the old-school parade to make it exciting for a new generation? Would old-timers still enjoy it? Why or why not?

966. In Culpepper, Virginia, one July 4th tradition is the annual Greased Pig Chase. The person who catches the slippery swine wins a prize. How might such an event go over in your house and why?

967. One of the best places to view fireworks in the country during the festivities is Mount Rushmore, in South Dakota. How would you feel if someone carved your likeness into a mountain? What would your friends think and why?

968. Another Independence Day staple is a good, old-fashioned barbecue. Imagine that you had to entertain a group of vegans during the meat-friendly holiday. What would you cook and how would you still feel patriotic about the whole thing?

969. The United States contains several island territories, such as the U.S. Virgin Islands, and they celebrate the holiday just as much as it's celebrated on the mainland. What would it be like to celebrate July 4th on a tropical island? How would it be different and why?

970. Describe what it might be like to experience Independence Day 100 years in the future. How do you think traditions would change? Why would some of the methods of celebration become outdated?

971. Imagine that the United States was never freed from the British. What would it be like to still be part of a colony that was ruled from afar? How might the laws be different? Why might you feel differently about your heritage?

972. In a distant possible future, all fireworks have been made into digital holograms. While the displays have become brighter, bolder and more high-definition, they are no longer real. What do you think such artificial explosions would lose by being faked? Which would you prefer, digital or real, and why?

973. You and your friends have decided to declare your independence and start a new country. What points might you try to make in this declaration? How would your new country alter the way people are treated? What would your new nation be called and why?

974. Independence Day is about freedom, but even after the Revolutionary War there were plenty of people who still weren't free. Why do you think slavery was still a part of early America? How do you think slaves felt with their masters talking about freedom and independence and why?

975. After opening a random book in the library, you've found out that one of your relatives was friends with the founding fathers of the nation. What did this ancestor of yours do with George Washington, Thomas Jefferson, and others? How was he or she involved with the creation of the United States?

976. What is your favorite 4th of July barbecue activity, other than eating? Why do you enjoy it so much?

977. You have been transported hundreds of years in the past to the Revolutionary War. You have been given an American flag to keep safe during the battle for independence. What do you do with the symbol of our nation to keep it safe? How do you avoid capture and keep yourself out of harm's way?

978. You are the Declaration of Independence, a piece of parchment in a museum that witnessed some of the greatest moments of our nation's beginning. What are some of the stories you could tell? What secrets might you know that historians left out?

979. Do you think it's important to remember how the United States of America was started as a country? Why or why not? What benefits might we gain from remembering our past?

980. How do you think people will look at the founders of the United States far, far in the future? Will they still be celebrated as heroes? Why or why not?

981. While many people love to watch and listen to exploding fireworks on Independence Day, some take a quieter approach by attending patriotic classical music concerts. Which would you rather experience on July 4th and why?

982. On the 4th of July, competitive eaters from around the world try to eat as many hot dogs as they can in Coney Island, Brooklyn, New York. Why do you think hot dog eating has become a competitive sport? Do you think it's gross or cool and why?

983. In the Declaration of Independence, Thomas Jefferson said that all people have the right to the pursuit of happiness. What do you think that means? How have you pursued happiness and why?

984. Imagine that your family held the largest local fireworks display in your neighborhood. How would you gather the fireworks together and what would people think of your family's patriotic and explosive actions? Why?

985. John Hancock became famous for being the first person to sign the Declaration of Independence. What do you think you might become famous for? Why?

986. Why do you think barbecues are so popular on Independence Day? If you could replace barbecue with another type of food during the holiday, what would it be and why?

987. The American Revolutionary War was difficult, and at several points it looked like we might lose the battle. How would the United States be different if it was never able to gain its independence? Why?

988. Even though the Declaration of Independence asserted that all people were created equal, there are continuing issues of inequality in the United States. What do you think it will take for people to actually be treated equally? When might such equality be achieved and why?

989. Describe a conversation between Thomas Jefferson and a colonist who was opposed to independence in 1776. How would Jefferson counteract the colonist's argument? Would Jefferson prevail at convincing the colonist? Why or why not?

990. Imagine that you have found one of the original copies of the Declaration of Independence in your attic. How did such an important document end up in your house? What will you do with it and why?

RAMADAN

991. Ramadan is a summer Muslim holiday in which people abstain from eating and drinking from dawn until sunset for an entire month. How would the observance of such a holiday impact your life? What might some of the difficulties be to keep up with it and why?

992. Also during the day, participants in Ramadan are supposed to avoid sinful behavior and speech. How successful do you think you'd be at doing the right thing and expressing kindness for an entire month straight during the day? What positive habits might you learn and why?

993. Ramadan is a holiday of self-control and self-discipline. What is a time that you had to exercise these traits? What do you think are the benefits of self-discipline and why?

994. Muslims observing Ramadan eat a pre-fast meal before the sun comes up called Suhoor. If you knew you weren't going to eat until sundown, what would you eat as your Suhoor and why? Would it be tough for you to get up early enough to get a meal in before sunrise?

995. Prayer is a major part of Ramadan. Do you think that prayer is an important part of a person's life? Why or why not?

996. Imagine that you overheard a friend or classmate praying for something that you might be able to help with. Would you try to help this person? Why or why not? If so, would you help the person anonymously or would you come out and tell him or her you were helping? Why?

997. Ramadan is meant to give observers a chance to reflect, especially on the plight of those less fortunate. For that reason, charity is a major activity during the holiday. If you had enough money and time to donate to charity, how would you use those resources and why? Why might one charity be more important to you than another?

998. Fasting is a part of other religions as well and is observed by the Jews on the holiday Yom Kippur. Why do you think fasting is an important event in multiple religions? What can one learn from fasting and why?

999. Imagine that you had to celebrate Ramadan on the same day as your birthday. You would not be able to eat cake or cupcakes brought in during class to celebrate. How might this be difficult for you? How would the meaning of your special day change?

1000. At the end of Ramadan, Muslims celebrate with the Eid ul-Fitr, a festival to break the fast. Have you ever celebrated a month-long accomplishment? If so, what was it and how did you commemorate your success? If not, write a story about succeeding at a major goal and celebrating its achievement with all of your friends.

ABOUT THE AUTHOR

Bryan Cohen's philosophy is to turn a few ideas into many. This concept was one of the reasons behind his passion of creating thousands of creative writing prompts. His books, including his best-seller *1,000 Creative Writing Prompts: Ideas for Blogs, Scripts, Stories and More*, have sold over 15,000 copies. Build Creative Writing Ideas, a website created by Bryan which contains hundreds of articles of writing advice, helps over 25,000 people a month to get over writers block and come up with new creative projects.

Bryan also writes about comedy, self-help and embarrassing anecdotes from his life. He is also an actor, director and producer who enjoys dabbling in both theatre and film in Chicago, Illinois. Bryan graduated from the University of North Carolina at Chapel Hill in 2005 with degrees in English and Dramatic Art with a minor in Creative Writing.

Bryan has published 20 books and plays.

Made in the USA
Monee, IL
22 June 2025

19813441R00059